How to Analyze People

&

Utilize Manipulation

The Face Whisperer - Learn How to Understand Secrets Hidden in the Human Face and Know More about Your Relationships through Dark NLP and Body Language

Henry Wood

The information in the following pages is broadly considered a truthful and accurate account of facts and as such, any inattention, use, or misuse of the information in question by the reader will render any resulting actions solely under their purview. There are no scenarios in which the publisher or the original author of this work can be in any fashion deemed liable for any hardship or damages that may befall them after undertaking information described herein.

Additionally, the information in the following pages is intended only for informational purposes and should thus be thought of as universal. As befitting its nature, it is presented without assurance regarding its prolonged validity or interim quality. Trademarks that are mentioned are done without written consent and can in no way be considered an endorsement from the trademark holder.

Table of Contents

CHAPTER ONE

HOW TO ANALYZE PEOPLE

Perceiving other people's feelings and thoughts is an important skill that helps you navigate interpersonal relationships. Every human being is different, but we are all wired the same way at the core level. Here, we start by recognizing subtle clues for a moment.

1. Establish baseline

I know people. To be able to read someone really, you need to know them well. Knowing someone personally makes you understand more about what their likes and dislikes are, what their common habits are, and what is not necessarily "spoken."

- Based on one person's opinion as well as some encounters with others.
- For example, you might have a friend who is generally very shy. If so, their fear may not be a sign of lies or tension. When you meet them on the street, common sense makes them nervous or anxious. Disagreeable. They have exciting feet.
- Pay attention to the habits of others. Do they always maintain eye contact? Does their voice change when they are nervous? How do they react when they are crazy? This will lead you to what you are looking for when trying to read them.

Ask open-ended questions. When you are reading someone, you are watching and listening. What you are not doing is to grab the conversation at the corner and guide it in your direction. So ask your question and get out of there. Sit down, relax, and enjoy the show.

- Open-ended questions allow them to speak more so that they can talk longer.

- It is best to ask for appropriate questions. Asking "How is your family?" may give you a messy response that doesn't help you to evaluate better the information you are looking for. You may be able to collect more personal information from "What book are you currently reading?"

Look for baseline conflicts. Something is happening to an ordinarily loving person who doesn't seem physically present and doesn't want to get close to anyone within a 10-foot stick. The same behavior Boo Radley shows does not necessarily mean the same thing. If you collect how people behave in daily life, be aware of things that do not engage.

- If something seems to be missing, you need to ask why, at least initially. They may be exhausted, had a fight with their significant other, got angered by their boss, or have a small personal problem they are stuck in. Do not assume that it reflects your relationship with that person before you know all the details.

Work with the cluster. Looking at a single clue is not a reason to jump to a conclusion. After all, someone may be leaning on you just because the chair is not comfortable.

- Try to get clues from their words, tone, body, and face. If you get one from each and have a lineup of all of them, it's safe to continue. But of course, a good way to check if you are right is to just ask directly.

Please know your weaknesses. As a mere human being, you can be mistaken. If you see something pretty, you will like it. If you are wearing a finely tailored Italian suit, they will probably trust you.

Humans generally think of dangerous people as those who are drunk, walking around the street, and carrying knives. In reality, most psychopaths are attractive and look well put together. Note that it is virtually impossible to control, but if it is not necessarily the best or most accurate thing, the subconscious tells you to judge the book by the cover.

SECRETS OF PSYCHOLOGISTS TO READ PEOPLE AS IF THEY WERE OPEN BOOKS

Surely you have wished more than once to be able to read other people's minds. Some are saved with the help of their developed intuition, but if you are not so perceptive, you only have one way out: learn to decipher body language.
It is no longer a secret that with the help of nonverbal communication we get 55 percent of the information. Allan Pease, the famous Australian writer mentioned it more than once. Expressions of the face, gestures and body movements can remove the mask from anyone, revealing their true thoughts and feelings.
The wording of Genial Guru proposes us to pay attention to the signals sent to us by the people around us without even knowing it.

1. **Closing the eyes**
    If a person, speaking with you, closes his eyes, you have to know that he is trying to hide or protect himself from the outside world. This does not mean that he fears you. Rather, it is the other way around. He wants to take you out of his field of vision. You may have bored him already. Close his eyes and bam! You have disappeared.

2. **Protecting the mouth by hand**
    It is a vivid example that we all have from childhood. Remember how you covered your mouth with the palm of your hand when you didn't want to say something. An adult is the same. Some fingers, palm or fist help us contain the words. Sometimes we mask it with a feigned cough.

3. **Biting the ring of your glasses**
    Is a friend of yours thoughtfully biting the rings of his glasses? Try to support and encourage him. Surely he will be worried about something and at his subconscious level try to feel safe, as in childhood with the mother's breast. By the way, a pencil, pen, finger, cigarette or even chewing gum in the mouth also indicate the same.

4. Showing face

Many women use this gesture to attract the attention of men. Supporting the chin on folded hands, we expose our face to show it, as if it were the shop window in a store, as if we were saying: "Here I am, so pretty, admire me." Men should remember this gesture so as not to miss the opportunity to make a compliment on time.

5. Stroking the chin

In this way the person tries to make a decision. At the same time, his gaze can be directed down, up, to the left or any other side. He does not realize what he sees at that precise moment, since he is completely immersed in his thoughts.

6. Crossed arms

It is one of the most common gestures. It is not surprising that many people feel very comfortable with this pose, since this gesture helps to isolate them from others. Many times we use it when we are not comfortable with something. Crossed arms are a clear sign of the negative attitude of your interlocutor.

7. Exposing oneself

This pose is more open. When a woman wants a man to like her, she starts exposing herself by showing her best sides. She straightens to highlight her breasts and crosses her legs. Folded arms are a clear signal of attention towards the interlocutor.

8. Leaning forward

When a person feels sympathy for his interlocutor and wants to have contact with him or her, he usually leans forward. At the same time, the feet may remain in the same place, but the body advances instinctively.

9. Leaning back

If the person leans against the back of his seat, he makes it clear that he is bored with the conversation. You may feel uncomfortable in the presence of your interlocutor.

10. Toe, heel

Yes, adults do too. Not only children. This gesture indicates that the person is very worried.

11. Rubbing his hands

It is said that the hands convey what the head thinks. When we rub our hands, we usually express expectations or hope of some success in something. In other words, we make this gesture when we think about future benefits.

12. Handshake "glove"

If your interlocutor greeting you grabs you with both hands, it shows that you can trust him.

13. Squeeze with palm up

The palm-up, covering the interlocutor's hand, indicates empathy, but only if done at once. If the hands were already held for a certain moment and then someone put the palm of the hand up, it may indicate their desire to show who is in charge.

14. Squeeze with palm down

By supporting your caller's hand, it is as if you were talking about your willingness to help him.

15. Squeeze with a touch

With the available hand the person can touch the forearm, elbow or the back of the person he is greeting. This invasion of personal space shows the need for communication. And the closer the body is, the greater the need.

16. Straightening the tie

Here everything depends on the situation. If it is a man who does it in the presence of a woman, it is highly possible that he likes her. But this gesture can also mean that the person does not feel comfortable. You might have lied or just want to leave.

17. Collecting non-existent hairs

It is thus called the gesture of repression. Most of the time people use it to express their tacit disagreement. In other words, they do not openly express their opinion, but they certainly do not agree with what is happening around them.

18. **Feet on the table**

This gesture can mean many things: bad manners, disrespect, desire to show off as a great boss or concern for your health. However, psychologists tend to believe that even if you feel very comfortable in this position, it would be better if you use it at home or in the presence of your family.

19. **Riding the chair**

A chair is not a horse and its back, although in some ways it seems, is not a shield. In addition, it was made for other purposes. So many people are bothered by this way of sitting around, because at the intuitive level we feel a lot of aggression from the "mounted" person. Normally, dominant people use this position.

20. **Playing with the shoe**

Cross-legged is one of the most attractive female poses. And if we add playing with the shoe half removed, we accentuate it even more. This gesture speaks of a relaxed and calm mood and serves as a kind of green light for a man.

21. **Eye contact**

The eyes are the mirror of the soul and a perfect instrument of communication. There we can read all the feelings and emotions of the interlocutor. Lovers stare into each other's eyes, unconsciously waiting to see how they get bigger. And this shows a lot, because the pupils can increase in size up to 4 times, compared to their normal state. And, by the way, if the person gets angry, their eyes become like accounts due to the maximum reduction of the pupils.

HOW TO ANALYZE A PERSON BY THEIR PHOTOS

Have you just met someone who added you to their Facebook, Twitter or Instagram and are you wondering what kind of personality they have? Do you want to know what message you give the world with your photographs on social networks? Since the arrival of the Internet in our lives, the way we relate with others has changed radically. Now we have space where others can see what we want them to see. The images we decide to upload to our social networks show much more than we imagine, an Internet profile is a projection of what we want to show the world, our desires and even our insecurities. That is why by making a correct analysis of the published photos, we can develop an accurate personality profile.
Tell me what profile picture you have and I will tell you who you are.

What the profile photos indicate
When we choose a profile picture (whether for WhatsApp, Facebook, Instagram...) we are choosing our cover letter to the world. After that election there is a series of mental processes that arise to avoid giving an image that we don't want to give. For example, someone more introverted will have more difficulties in this process and may not change their photographs very often. In extreme cases, these people hide behind anonymous profiles.

Some elements that we can analyze from profile photos are the following:
- **Pose:** People who are not afraid to expose themselves usually put out open arms, calm and full-length (or half-body) photographs, however, a more reserved person probably has a more serious photograph, with arms crossed and in a more closed plane.
- **Facial expression:** An open smile, without touch-ups and head-on; they are usually self-confident, open and outgoing people. A grimace may be a sign that they want to show "naturalness" but, deep down, they feel insecure and force themselves to be funny in a photograph. The most serious people (or those who use their networks for professional purposes) usually leave with a half-smile or, with a sober expression.

15

- **If they go out with people:** Going out with many people in the photo can indicate a tendency to be sociable, they enjoy life more in the company of others and a photo of them alone does not represent them.
- **If it is a photo with their partner:** Although the image we give on social networks about our partner is not reality, uploading many photos or having a profile picture with your partner does not imply anything bad, on the contrary. A photo with our partner means that we have taken the step of showing the world who we are united with and who is part of our life.
- **If it is an old or childhood photo:** These types of images indicate a strong anchor to the past, we may be going through a bad time and do not want to connect with it or, we are simply afraid to move on in our lives.
- **Photo color:** Color is also a very important element, a black and white photo can be a sign of a melancholic, poetic or introverted personality. On the other hand, bright colors usually express vitality and joy.
- **If the photo is not of us:** There are people who hide behind anonymous profiles, avatars of soccer players, celebrities or cartoons. These individuals travel through the networks without interest to show their personality, either because of fear, insecurities or because they do not like to show their lives to a very wide audience.

The psychology of colors in profile photos

The study of how colors affect our lives has also reached the analysis of personality, the tones we choose for our virtual presentation letter also show very characteristic features of us.

Black and white photos

As we have commented previously, a black and white photo can be a sign of melancholy and artistic tendencies. Retouching a photograph with the objective of removing the shades can also indicate bad self-esteem and, as a consequence, certain insecurity when showing ourselves to the world.

Photos with lots of colors

Strident photos, with many shades and full of color are characteristics of equally strident and striking people. Not only is it a sign of extraversion, but the striking colors also indicate the desire to attract attention and to have a certain presence in the lives of others, whether in the real world or on the Internet.

Photos with blue tones
Using cold tones such as blue can indicate two things: either a corporate personality, sober and elegant or a tendency to be a cold and calculating person. These tones do not invite you to delve into the personal depths of each one.

Photos with red color
If this striking tone predominates in the photo, we may want to show the energy and passion we have in our day to day. The use of warm colors denotes an intense, competitive and sometimes aggressive personality.

Half-face photos: meaning
Not showing our face partially can indicate two very different things:
- **Mysterious personality:** Half-face invites you to enter the profile to discover more, see what that person hides and reveal his personality.
- **Disinterest in social networks:** A person who does not mind being exposed in social networks but, however, does not want to waste time on them. For this type of individuals, a half-face photo implies that they have given the message that yes that Facebook profile is theirs, but they also do not want to show their whole life on it.

Back photo: Meaning
It is possible that in the profile picture we do not even want to face the camera. Back photos reflect a certain level of resistance when having social networks and being active in them. In this type of photos the face is not visible and, therefore, we hide our facial expressions from the world of the Internet.
On the other hand, a photo from behind can also mean that we have gone through a painful time and that, right now, we do not have enough courage to show ourselves in the face of a world as extensive as social networks.

Finally, it is worth mentioning that, although it is interesting to know how to analyze a person by their photos, each individual is a world, a very intricate set of experiences and paths and that it is better to talk to a person if we want to know them thoroughly.

FIVE MAJOR FACTORS ANALYZING PERSONALITY, ACCORDING TO GOLDBERG

Lewis Goldberg's personality theory is also known as the "Big Five Model." It stems from a variety of studies in which the excellence of a particular personality trait is repeated as a factor determining people's way of life. It was in 1993 that it was structured as a theory.
The five main personality traits are identified by capital letters and are also known as "main factors". The first is the element of "O" —openness to new experiences. The second is the responsibility of "C". The third is "E" or extrovert. The fourth is "A" or kind. And finally, the fifth is "N" or emotional instability. The letters from the acronym "OCEAN".

> *"Each one is like a god, but you can leave it to God."*

> *-Miguel Servet-*

Similarly, each of these characteristics is made up of more specific characteristics. From this model, a variety of personality tests have been developed that can evaluate and measure how people have evaluated. Let's take a closer look at the features and characteristics of the model.

Openness to experience, one of the personality traits
Openness to experience ("O") refers to the ability to find new skills, space them in life and creatively visualize the future. Those who have this level at a high level are imaginative people who appreciate art and collaborate with others. They are also curious and prefer variations over every day.

The opposite is people who have closed to an experience they have never experienced before. The opposition characterizes them. This means that they prefer a guaranteed traditional one. They prefer strict routines because they take time to adapt to new things. They tend to be technical and tend to show little interest in abstraction.

Responsibility or factor "C"

This dimension relates to self-control ability and the ability to develop effective ways of acting. It relates to the ability to plan, organize and execute tasks. You must also be able to achieve your goals, keep to time, and maintain your goals.
People with high scores in this dimension are often seen as organized, reliable and demanding people. Taking this personality trait to extremes can lead to over-perfectionism and even work addiction. They feel a great need to succeed.

Extraversion, another personality trait

It has to do with having fun in other people's companies. People who have this most prominent feature feel comfortable when they are with others and act in harmony when they are in a group. They are good people working in teams, optimistic and enthusiastic. Along with others, they are like sea fish. There is an introverted person on the other side, and they prefer to work alone. Often, they feel certain distrust and attention to others. They prefer a small circle of friends and are very uncomfortable with a large group.

"A" factor: kindness

Mainly related to empathy. Those who show excellence in this personality factor understand, forgive and are calm with others. They demonstrate their ability to understand other people's needs and feelings.
The people on the other side are in conflict. These are people who like discussion and debate and want to give their own perspective. Hostility is their brand. They can work well in activities that require demonstrations of competition and energetic attitudes towards others.

Emotional instability or neurosis

It specifically talks about the ability or lack of ability that one has to overcome in the face of difficult life situations. People who show a high level of this factor are characterized by unpredictable behavior. They do not maintain a series of actions, but the reasons are not very clear and their reactions are different.

At the opposite end, there are stable people who remain attentive and modest in critical situations. They are quiet people who are relieved with the ability to handle difficulties and mistakes. Their emotional state is positive, even in the face of difficulties.

READ PEOPLE AND SEE-THROUGH

Honestly, wouldn't it be nice to be able to assess people with lightning speed and to know immediately how to deal with the best? Which buttons do you have to press to reach what you want?

You know instantly which kind of person you are dealing with and which behavior is likely to happen to you from a few perceptions. This knowledge gives you a huge informational edge, while the other person is still completely in the dark, not knowing the number of inferences on their personality you have already learned.

Your ability to perceive what others have missed reading between the lines, after a few sentences, will allow you to get a clear picture of a person and place them in a grid that will allow you to predict the person's remaining attributes and preferences. In short, you can read people and see what really drives them.

Wouldn't that be an incredibly helpful skill? Just think about the benefits this knowledge could bring you. In which situations would you have the decisive advantage? In which situations could you have prevented so much, if you had already known in advance, how a person would probably act? And with which people would it be much easier, if you knew exactly how you should deal with them?

We humans love to look for patterns in our environment and to recognize them.

Scientifically this tendency is called "Randomness Error." It is one of the automatically occurring attention mistakes that cause us to perceive the reality a bit distorted. In a nutshell, we assign meaning to random events that do not have any meaning. They just happened completely arbitrarily.

However, we try to make sense of everything and therefore recognize seemingly recurrent patterns that help us to categorize events in our environment. Even though these categories often do not exist. And of course we do the same with our fellow human beings and their behaviors. Of course, this has some advantages and disadvantages.

Classifying people into categories makes their behavior more manageable and allows us to rate the unknown. This seems to be an inherent pattern of human behavior. Evolutionary conditioning was necessary to detect dangers early. Today, it helps us to be better at dealing with people and to assess how they will behave. It allows us to be one step ahead of others.

Already in ancient Greece, the personality of the people was classified in the grid of the temperament theory. Similar to the personality types according to Carl Gustav Jung, the Myers-Briggs type indicator or the "Big 5" of the OCEAN model, which is often used in psychology today, people of every segment were given certain qualities.
By recognizing some of these typical behaviors or characteristics, people can be assigned to a segment. Once assigned, one knows which other behaviors and characteristics the classified person is now statistically most likely to have and how best to deal with it.
Of course, this knowledge has not only advantages, but also great disadvantages. Katja Vogt once said that in all the drawers that we humans entertain, unfortunately only a sock is lost.

This quote nicely reminds us that too hasty conclusions can often have consequences and many things pass us because of our now active expectation filter. We should therefore pay very close attention to whether the model used really allows us to assign other unerring drawers.

The models mentioned above have some upgradable points that need to be considered when trying to "categorize" people. We in the NLP are convinced that we can always only recognize tendencies. The world is not black and white, it shows in many shades. And so do personality traits of people.

The second point is that we humans have the ability to change and evolve. Such an analysis is static in nature. Just as an exam is just a snapshot, a survey or questionnaire can capture our personality at some point in time based on a set of criteria.

But because NLP itself is a dynamic model and we constantly calibrate our conversational waking ears and sharp eye in conversations and situations, we can easily perceive changes and deviant behavior.

NLP's behavioral analysis is always up-to-date, and its users are aware that human behavior is constantly changing, but they have the ability to respond flexibly to these changes.

Also, many analysis models overlook the fact that human behavior is very context-dependent. I can take the helm in a situation and lead a group safely to the desired point.

Likewise, in a different context, I can just sit back, wait and see what the others do, and talk and engage only when I have a clear picture of the situation. Just because I got things going in a context and was virtually the "doer" does not mean that I do that in any other context, let alone that it always makes sense. But how can I analyze and read people and their behavior with NLP?

The model we use is called MBC - Meta Behavioral Coding. It combines the best elements of some well tested and working analysis models.

These include, for example, the metaprogramming from the NLP, which is derived from it specifically for the working context of Dr. med. Rodger Bailey derived LAB® Profiles (Language and Behavior Profiles) and some analysis tools used in profiling and the military.

With MBC, we use a framework that allows us to incorporate human behavior into over 20 facets. On the basis of the different characteristics and metaprogram combinations, we can assess ourselves and our counterpart very precisely and derive action strategies.

One of the metaprograms of the VAKOG model tells you something. This metaprogram tells you from the language of a human in which sensory channels your counterpart perceives his environment and thus also in which sensory channels you should talk to this person in order to create a good basis for conversation and to prevent one another from talking to one another.

Metaprograms themselves are therefore unconscious personality patterns and filters of our brain. These determine our behavior, how we are motivated, how we make decisions, how we value things, and how we perceive our environment. Metaprograms thus help us to see how our counterpart is sorting his reality and what his subconscious personality patterns look like.

Of course, these patterns have a very strong impact on how and what we talk about. From the structure of a person's language, MBC allows us to create precisely those unconscious patterns to hear and to get insights into the personality. A small example. Markus and Christina have just a small disagreement at a meeting.

Markus says: "Before we start, we have to rethink our decisions and analyze together whether we have thought everything through. We cannot risk external factors bugging us."

Christina says: "Thinking even more does not make sense. We finally have to get started, we're running out of time. We will already be able to handle the external factors when the time comes."

Here different metaprogramming meets, which causes conflicts more frequently. We're talking about the meta-program Proactive / Reactive.

Proactive people are action-oriented and take initiative. They want to do something. The activity and the action are in the foreground. Precise analysis of the situation and the most accurate balancing of all available alternatives usually leave it to others. Much can only be considered for them once you have started. They assume that they have a handle on what happens and can influence environmental factors through their behavior.

In everyday life, they are often referred to as "makers," as they initiate many ideas and take the first steps. This is helpful when an action is required. In extreme cases, the quick start and initiate actions can also happen rashly and anger other people. It may seem that they act like "steamrolling" and could have prevented some with a little more thought in advance.

Reactive people to leave the initiative to other people. Situations have to "mature" for them to make decisions. They like to let things take their course in order to see what impact this has on them. Situations need to be understood and analyzed before an action is taken. Reactive people also need to be completely sure that they have considered all alternatives. They see themselves in the area of the tension of external influences and find that their behavior is influenced by environmental factors.

In everyday life, they are often referred to as "analyst" or "thinker." They provide valuable solutions and sharp analysis of problems. In extreme cases, this metaprogram can lead to an "analysis" loop, as there is always new input to analyze and understand.

There is no action at all until it is too late. Sometimes, other people also perceive reactive people as "passive" because they spend a lot of time waiting and contemplating. This can also make them passengers of their own lives.

So you realize that both Metaprograms have their advantages and disadvantages, none is better than the other. Depending on the situation or task, one expression can prove to be more advantageous than the other. Just ask yourself what expressions Mark and Christina have and how you can recognize them.

How do I know which characteristic my counterpart has?

Proactive:

Is very active in body language and movements. Linguistically noticeable by short, sometimes incomplete sentences. Has problems staying calm for a long time.

Typical sets of proactive people:
- What are we waiting for? Here we go!
- Now it's time to get started.
- Let's get started.

Reactive:
Tend to lean back more often or in a classic analysis posture. Speaks slowly and in longer, nested sentences. Longer inactive phrases are no problem.

Typical sentences of reactive persons:
- Let's look at exactly what we are dealing with here.
- We should think about that again before we do something.
- Let us also listen to other opinions on this topic.

How can I use these patterns?
Proactive people can be very well used as motivators and initiators of actions. They get things going and start where others are still thinking. But when there is a longer standstill, they become impatient and try to get things moving. They can help get an otherwise reactive team going and prevent over-analysis.
Reactive people are very good analysts, they weigh, want to understand and act thoughtfully. Especially in situations that need to be controlled in the background, or in an advisory capacity, it is recommended to use reactive persons. They can give proactive doers a clear direction and prevent important things from being overlooked in a hurry. While the other one is starting to work, they can analyze further in the background and gradually work out new input.

How can you best deal with proactive / reactive people?

If you realize in a group process that proactive members are getting impatient and getting started, but the more reactive ones do not feel ready and need more time, then you can intervene very simply in this process. Split tasks and share the group is the magic formula.

Give the proactive something to do. Let them either fulfill smaller sub-goals or tasks that have already been agreed or give them tasks that need to be done either way. With them you talk best about what has to be done. Once you've told them that, you do not have to worry about anything anymore, the tasks are done independently and quickly.

Thus, you give the reactive persons the time and opportunity to continue important analysis processes and give them the security they need. You allow them to understand that this process need to be carefully considered. With them too, it can help to use partial goals or milestones to make the analysis more precise and faster. Here it is important to set clear deadlines and execute them in order to prevent rethinking.

This way, the situation with Markus and Christina can easily be resolved. Both are focused on a common goal, and Christina can get started, while Markus can calmly devise strategies to tackle external factors. Of course, you explain their tasks to the two ineffective speech patterns that satisfy their metaprogramming.

Speech patterns that you can use to link to them include:
- **Christina:** Do, do, get started, act, now!
- **Markus:** Think, weigh, think, analyze, wait, act, when the time is right!

What brings you now MBC?
In a nutshell: you can read carefully from the language of your conversation partners and recognize what they need and how they tick. So you know how to explain something "brain-friendly" in their language so that it makes sense to them intuitively and sounds good. You do not have to rely on a static personality analysis, you have the ability to calibrate your opponent's tendencies with a proven and simple grid at any time and in any context, and so have clear action strategies for you.

Imagine, you are in a discussion and know what arguments will convince. In a negotiation, you realize how your demands are being accepted. What if you have to sell something and know exactly how to raise the need for it? Whether you want to motivate, lead, understand or respond to someone, you will notice a noticeable difference and be able to prevent much in advance.

HOW TO INFLUENCE PEOPLE

When we need to convince someone, we can use many techniques. Obviously if we make a good proposal, we have valid arguments and what we want to do is a win-win, it will be easy to convince our interlocutor of our interests.
But apart from the content, there are some small tricks that we can use to influence the people we talk to and achieve our goals.
The way we talk, our attitude and knowing how to handle the conversation can be the key to getting a favorable response in our interest.

1. **Smile**
   A smile on your face is the first thing you have to do if you want to influence people. When someone smiles, it conveys happiness and we all like to feel good. When a proposal is made with a smile on their face, we are more predisposed to accept what they are asking.

2. **Take advantage of fatigue**
   When we are tired, we don't feel like arguing, and we are more willing to say yes (even if they leave us alone).
   Cults know this perfectly. Therefore, the sessions where you are "brainwashed" are always long and exhausting. They know that a tired person has low defenses and is more willing to obey and accept that what you are saying is true.

3. **Make the ball**

The ego is one of the weak points of all people. We all like to be told how good we are, and we are more willing to serve a person who makes us feel good. It is not easy to flatter without them noticing. So, if you're complimenting someone to convince him, do it in a subtle and credible way.

4. Tell him many times YES

If you want to influence someone, make them say yes. When in a conversation, and we say yes many times, our brain understands that we are in tune with the person with whom we speak. The inertia of responding can be a good tool to get us to respond affirmatively to what we want.

Cold-door commercials are one of the strategies they use very often:

- Do you want the best for your family? Yes
- Do you like to save on the fixed expenses of your home? Yes
- Do you live in this address? Yes
- Do you like things to work correctly? Yes
- Do you want me to make a special offer for you? Yes

Make the ball roll and make them say yes many times are two of the basic techniques of commercials.

5. Do not take the reason from your interlocutor

Showing someone that he is not right in what he says is a good strategy to feel good and have the feeling of "having won the argument."
But it is not a good strategy to influence another person.
When we argue, most of the time we end up curling ourselves even more in the position we defend.
If you want to influence another person, you better not discuss and ignore the negative arguments of the other person (this strategy is one used by all politicians).

6. Extra trick: Use your voice well

The voice is a key element, when it comes to influencing others.

There are 4 aspects of the voice to consider. These four elements, which make us perceive a certain voice differently, are; intensity, tone, timbre and duration. On the union of all parties, it will depend on a voice being more or less persuasive. The ideal formula to be persuasive with our voice would be like that; medium-strong intensity, serious tone, open bell and medium-fast duration.

CHAPTER TWO

THE IMPORTANCE OF UNDERSTANDING YOURSELF

Alexander the Great said: Knowing yourself is the most challenging task, as it not only stimulates our rationality directly but also tests our fear and passion. If you know yourself completely, you can understand the reality of others and their surroundings.

Self-knowledge and interpersonal intelligence
The Macedonian king was right. Because, through self-awareness, we learn to grow effectively in life and face everyday life faster. Knowing what we are, what we feel, and what we want to achieve is an ability related to interpersonal intelligence.

Having interpersonal intelligence means understanding who we are, knowing how to identify emotions, and acting accordingly. Skills that regulate behavior solve problems effectively and make decisions. Through self-awareness, we learn to recognize our abilities and limitations. This allows you to plan your goals more realistically and avoid future frustrations. People with interpersonal intelligence know how to master their emotions and adapt to their situation.

The enhancement of interpersonal intelligence is to know yourself
Is it possible to improve interpersonal intelligence? If you are interested in knowing yourself and growing inward, you can run a series of exercises that will help you leverage this intelligence.
Control your emotions: This is the skill you need to work with. Control means knowing how to act based on one emotion and not another emotion. Learn how to identify negative emotions and make them positive. For example, if you feel angry, think about why you are angry and try to redirect. A very effective tip is to laugh at trivia. This feature helps to turn negative emotions into positive emotions.

Travel inside. Erich Fromm says, "Self-awareness begins with self-acceptance. Accept yourself. You will know each other better." Make a list of your virtues and shortcomings. Ask nearby people to do the same and know what images people have of you. Compare both lists and improve what you don't like.

Please practice it. Observe how emotions affect mood and look for ways to turn negative things into positive ones. Write down your bad behavior on paper and think about how to solve it. For example, how can you change your feelings when you become sad? Talk to a friend? Please practice it.

Accept yourself: Jean-Jaques Rousseau said, "If they don't thank themselves, no one can be happy." Analyze what your abilities and limits are. Set short-term and medium-term goals accordingly. This will strengthen your self-esteem and teach you to accept that you are yourself. A great exercise to get to know yourself.

Understanding: Please note what you feel throughout the day. Morning, noon, night, when waking up, and before going to bed. Find out what is causing these emotions.

BENEFITS OF PERSONAL SELF-KNOWLEDGE

If you ask us if we know ourselves, we will answer without hesitation. After all, we are live with ourselves for 24 hours and no one knows us better than us. But that knowledge is a mirror that looks at us, where the reputation and appreciation of others want to find their own image, what we think we are or we are soaked in.
By doing so, you can grow without really getting to know yourself. I believe that I know myself, if not, I will continue to build on this self-knowledge first. In order to achieve this, reach your own true objective personal knowledge, as this may limit the full development of your life, and especially if the evaluation is negative it is essential to do.

Reflect to get to know each other better

For this, it is essential to spend time on objective and critical (but not self-destructive) reflections that allow us to understand both our qualities and defects. You have to do it objectively, that is, without negatively evaluating the weaknesses you find in yourself. Knowledge is the first step to change, and without knowledge, we cannot improve ourselves.

Self-knowledge to know our feelings

Self-awareness also enables us to really know how we feel.

Know what you want from life

Knowing yourself can tell you what you want and what you don't want in your life. This is an essential requirement to be happy because you can understand the steps and the direction to achieve your goals.

SELF CONCEPT

How can I know who I am? What is the process of creating and maintaining an image?

Knowledge can help you decide what to think and what to do in every situation. This self-awareness can occur at the individual or group level. Recognizing our identity and the identity of others promotes our lives and promotes our interpersonal and group relationships.

Personality psychologists have worried about the identity content itself. Social psychologists, on the other hand, have paid more attention to the way in which people think about things that affect their behavior and to the influence that they can have in their interpersonal and intergroup relationships.

On the other hand, personality psychologists have focused on looking for typologies of people while social psychologists have become more interested in looking for general processes that can affect all individuals.

SELF-CONCEPT
What is the self-concept?
It is the idea or image that the individual has of himself.
The global self-concept of a person is formed by the different roles he plays which may vary over time or create new ones.

Descriptions on what is the self-concept:

- Like the whole person in general.
- All parts of the personality of an individual.
- Collection of skills, goals, values, etc. that distinguish people.
- Personality of the individual.
- Subjective experiences.
- Beliefs about oneself.

Knowing oneself: self-knowledge
Self-knowledge is the understanding of who you are and what your goals and abilities are. To reach that understanding, we turn to self-schemes.

The self-concept is formed by a large number of self-schemes that help us in the face of negative events. A person who is unemployed can develop a negative self-scheme (being a failure), but if that same person considers that he has a good family relationship, he will resort to his self-scheme of a good father to have a better opinion of himself.

Extreme self-schemes can produce negative consequences for the individual.

How can we get to know who we are?
Making inferences about our behavior
Self-awareness theory: People build their own concepts by creating internal attributes of their actions. We assign personal characteristics that explain why we behave as we do.
The attribution we make is subject to change by external agents. Also, if someone uses rewards or punishment to perform a task that is already intrinsically motivated, people re-assign the reason for doing it to an external source rather than explaining the internal cause. This is called the over justification effect.

Comparing ourselves to others
Social comparison (Festinger): Comparison made by people of their opinions and abilities with those of other members of the group to which they belong. It occurs at the individual and intergroup level. It is much related to social cognition.
Shine with the glory of others. Ally with desirable people or groups for some reason to improve the impression that others have of oneself.

How is the self-concept formed and modified?
    a)   **The theory of self- discrepancy:** People are motivated to maintain a coherence between the beliefs and perceptions we have about ourselves. When differences occur, we feel uncomfortable and try to reduce dissonance.

This theory postulates other different self-concepts that guide…

Functions of the guides:
1. They are incentives for our future behavior.
2. They operate as a criterion for comparing our real self-concept. What are these other self-concepts?
   - Ideal self-concept: How we would like to be.
   - Responsible self-concept: How we think we should be.
   - Potential self-concept: How we think we can become.
   - Expected self-concept: How we expect to be in the future.

All these self-concepts can be considered from our point of view and from the point of view of some other significant person for us.

Five assumptions on which the theory of self-contradiction is based:
1. We are trying to bring our true self-concept closer to other self-concepts.
2. Self-contradiction is a cognitive structure that correlates with different types of self-concepts.
3. Contradictions between different types of self-concepts cause different negative psychological situations associated with specific emotional/motivational states.

4. The probability that self-contradiction creates psychological distress depends on the ease with which it is activated in a person's mind.
5. The greater the magnitude and accessibility of a kind of self-contradiction for an individual, the more discomfort associated with that kind of self-contradiction.

Reasons that affect knowledge about oneself
Self-assessment
It is the reason that leads us to seek information about ourselves and review all the components that are part of our self-concept: skills, limitations, beliefs, etc.

There are two views:
1. One more focused on the positive or negative assessment of the self (self-esteem).
2. Another in which the degree to which circumstances, contexts, and situation influence the evaluation that people make of themselves is taken into account.

Self-assessment is greatly influenced by the affective state, and that influence is mutual.
1. To think that we are not intelligent can make us unhappy.
2. If we are depressed, we can believe that we will not pass an exam.

Three strategies for maintaining positive self-assessment:
*   **Through social comparisons:** If you feel unwell, comparing yourself to the person below makes you feel better.
*   **Through reducing uncertainty:** Activating self-concept and its self-assessment creates uncertainty about what we really are, and comparing it with others can be reduced.
*   **About expressing value:** Expressing value provides a tool to know each other. Self-affirmation is one example, and it is about expressing our needs, desires, and opinions.

Self-check
It is the motivation to confirm the image we have of ourselves.

Self-verification theory: We like to be seen by others as we see ourselves. We like others to tell us that we are the way we think we are. It is a search for consistency.

To achieve behavioral coherence, three strategies are used:
- Look for an interaction.
- Show clear signs of identity.
- Increase your efforts to elicit self-confirming information, such as requesting feedback.

To achieve coherence in a cognitive way, we develop a perception of reality compatible with how we see ourselves. Three strategies are used:
- By selective attention
- By selective memory
- By careful interpretation

Strategic self-verification: Individuals prefer to perceive them better than they perceive themselves.

The evaluative component of self-knowledge: self-esteem
Self-esteem is the attitude of the individual towards himself. It is about the assessment that the person does of everything that is included in their self-concept along a positivity-negativity dimension.

Self-esteem as a thermometer of group acceptance
The search for positive self-esteem is related to the basic social motive of personal empowerment (every human being's need to feel special and happy with himself).

In individualistic cultures, there will be a tendency to self-encouragement while in collectivist cultures, its members will feel better if they become a worthy member of the group.

There is a hypothesis about the possible evolutionary origin of this need: the reason for personal empowerment drove our ancestors to reduce the probability of being ignored or rejected by other people and to avoid social exclusion. When there was any indication of rejection by the group, self-esteem would decrease, and the threatened person would look for the problem that has jeopardized their membership to correct it.

In this way, self-esteem would act as a "sociometer" and its high or low level would not be because individuals were happy or not with themselves, but because they managed to maintain membership in social groups.

Characteristics of people with high and low self-esteem.

People with high self-esteem:
- Persistent and resistant to failure.
- Emotionally stable.
- Less flexible and malleable.
- Less easily influenced and more difficult to persuade.
- It is not a conflict to want and obtain success and approval - Positively react to a happy and successful life.

Thorough, with a stable and consistent self-concept - Motivated to self-improvement.

People with low self-esteem:
- Vulnerable to the impact of daily situations.
- Very changing in terms of emotions and mood.
- Flexible and malleable.
- Easy to persuade and influence.
- They want success and approval but are skeptical about it - React negatively to life cheerful and successful.
- With an inconsistent and unstable self-concept.
- With a self-protective motivation.

CHAPTER THREE

HOW TO ANALYZE YOUR RELATIONSHIP

While relationships are complex, they do not necessarily have to be difficult as long as they are evaluated. In order for them to be healthy, it is enough that both members work on their insecurities, separate previous bad experiences and strengthen empathy.
Being affectionate, communicating correctly with our partner, having a good level of sexual desire, developing the capacity for consensus, being willing to solve problems, respect each other, set goals together and balance our individuality with life as a couple are the main factors that The Nicolás Moreno Clinical Psychology Center, in Granada-Spain, underlines as the fundamentals for a couple to succeed.

Now, regardless of the time we have with our partner, it is important that we periodically evaluate our relationship, in order to analyze the positive and negative before a small problem grows. Prevention is always better than regret.

Relationships are dynamic, in fact, experts say that this dynamism is that which allows the courtship or marriage to evolve and its members to grow personally and as a team. Every union implies agreements that are by no means static, so permanent evaluation can help us reconsider approaches we may have made at the beginning of our relationship, but they are no longer working.

The doctor and counselor of couples, Monsita Nazario, argues that assessing the relationship can ensure the health and future of the union. The doctor even emphasizes that the direction taken by divergence and incompatibility, which appear over time, must be noted in order to make sound decisions regarding life in common.

Key points to assess the relationship
The specialist highlights three key points to consider when assessing the relationship:

Periodic Analysis:
Constantly assessing the relationship allows us to raise awareness, stay alert and make life as a couple a priority. Nazario recommends that this be done daily, because knowing that we are in the process of constant evaluation, we strive to do better and better and avoid becoming demotivated, neglected and tired. "Failure to follow up on the processes damages them and puts them at risk of failure," he says. In addition, it highlights that the periodic analysis should be considered as one of the fundamental agreements at the beginning of the relationship to be able to tackle the reasons that lead to distancing and separation in time.

Reinventing yourself is the key:
The success of a relationship is not proportional to how long it lasts; In fact, many years of life as a couple do not guarantee the thorough knowledge of both members.
Getting to know each other is a lifelong process, so the expert asserts that the key to happy couples is to grow and reinvent themselves based on the stage in which the relationship is, because conflicts cannot be avoided but its impact can be reduced with a timely evaluation.
To love is to be able to transform ourselves and each couple will do it in a different way; of course, the doctor emphasizes that the transformation must occur consciously and by both members to avoid dysfunctionality.

Love Maps:
Loving someone implies knowing him, so the counselor is precise that it is essential the couple know each other deeply: their tastes, history, concerns, manias, ways of thinking and postures on different issues.

They are the so-called "love maps" and you have to keep them up to date in order to handle the circumstances presented to them more effectively. In our evaluation, Nazario proposes an essential question: "What would it be like to be married to someone like me?"
The answer will undoubtedly make us more aware of the weaknesses and strengths we have and how to take care of them.

Likewise, the consultant warns of the existence of certain actions classified as "horsemen of the apocalypse": criticism, complaint, contempt, defensive attitude and evasion, which are present in every relationship, so our task is to warn them, stop them and neutralize them.

To do this, it is recommended to write monthly the purpose of life in common to stay connected.

On the other hand, the psychologist Miriam Martín invites us to ask ourselves the following questions to evaluate our relationship: Does this link add or subtract us? Does it help us to be better and develop as people? Does it limit us and generate negative emotions? Based on them we can measure how well we are going and decide what changes to make.

Keys to a healthy relationship
There are no partner schools, but there are many tools to learn, even informally, to have a relationship that provides us with well-being. That is why we include some keys to make this experience healthy:

- Avoid emotional dependence to maintain high self-esteem. Depending on the tastes and needs of the couple promotes distancing, that is why we must preserve our autonomy and maintain interest in work, friends, and hobbies. All this will balance the personal space with the shared one and will provide stability.
- Respect the privacy of the other, accept their decisions and way of being. Do not manipulate or pretend that you are changing, and it may be better to change ourselves, especially the perspective from which we see what bothers us about our partner.
- To be authentic, that is, not to be permanently trying to show our best version because it is unreal and more than generating closeness with the other will end up chasing them away. The true interest towards every human being is when we feel we have access to them when they show us their hidden aspects and emotions without shame.

- Communicating assertively is essential. Good communication can make a discussion constructive. We must talk a lot with our partner to strengthen the relationship and learn to negotiate without reproach or evasion. Listening carefully, understanding your point of view, letting you see that we understand what you have said and expressing our point of view in a friendly tone will allow us to find consensual solutions with which we will both win.
- Take care of the details to maintain the relationship. Say and do what at first generated so much happiness in the other and that due to lack of time or routine, we sometimes leave aside. Gestures should not diminish over time, on the contrary.
- Respect and trust the other. Jealousy will only bring us discomfort and make the relationship fail.
- Have common goals that generate interest and enthusiasm. This will avoid the monotony and boredom that both deteriorate life as a couple.
- Share quality time in doing what we enjoy together.
- Maintain social relationships to enrich our life and revitalize it.

Let us consider what works for us, for now, and we can evaluate ourselves and pay more attention to our relationship because it is one of the most important we have and it is always worth cultivating.

Powerful Questions
To analyze and strengthen your relationship:
- What do you admire about your partner?
- What do you think of your life partner?
- What has your partner contributed to your personal or professional achievements?
- What do you like about the way you are?
- What goals do you have together in five years?
- What things should improve in the relationship, according to your partner?
- What behaviors on your part may be destabilizing the relationship?
- What situations generate conflict between the two?
- What should happen in the relationship, so that everything is much better?

- What moments or behaviors would be worth recovering?
- What agreements would you like to propose to your partner?
- What has to happen for these common goals to be met?
- What can you do differently with your partner today?
- What recognition does your life partner deserve?
- What love story do you want to tell your children about their parents?

HOW TO UNDERSTAND IF MY BOYFRIEND CHEATS WITH ANOTHER WOMAN ON ME

Fear is one of the emotions that a relationship often creates. When the individual observes actual signs of this reality, even when the simple theory generates thoughts and emotions that generate distress present in the affected person, the fears associated with potential infidelity generate psychological wear. How do I know if my boyfriend and another woman are cheating on me?

Signs to know that another woman is cheating on you with your boyfriend
If you are affected regularly by the mental noise of doubt, it is because you have witnessed some gesture or action that causes you uneasiness. Try to take the time to think more closely, though, so an intuition that may be wrong does not get carried away.

Are you a jealous person?
With this chronic doubt, some individuals live because their relationship projects their inner reality. What are a jealous person's normal symptoms? He has been jealous of multiple partners, and this issue is the usual cause of many discussions. This episode of confusion, that is, is not isolated but recurrent. We present some tips in the following chapter to help you avoid being so jealous of your partner.

Has he lied

In some significant way to you?
In a person who fears the abandonment of the person he wants, doubts can generate a very negative inner discourse. Try to curb your mind not to make expected value judgments and focus on your level of confidence and contact in your relationship, given these internal doubts. For instance, on a scale of 0 to 5, rate what your judgment is on this relationship balance.

If you have noticed lies in your partner regularly or lack honesty in matters that have influenced you by recognizing the facts, the fact creates a predisposition to your doubt. On the contrary, this attribute represents a different mentality if your partner's actions have been characterized by habitual honesty.

Lies are not necessarily found immediately in a partnership. It is often a friend or someone outside the relationship who records any details that he didn't know about the protagonist. Have you witnessed some of this kind of situation?

Habitual Conduct
In a partnership, behaviors occur that represent the construction of a common life project. Try answering the following questions if you doubt your boyfriend's likelihood of cheating on you with another girl.

When did that question start to emerge inside you? What occurred? Try to focus on what the turning point in you was that caused this mood. Have you found some major shift in your partner's actions involving you and your life together?

Behavioral changes may influence various levels, e.g., cost level, calendar change, new leisure plans, new friendships, makeovers, lack of touch, or unnecessary mobile usage. In the existence of new partnerships, the importance of the shift in materialized behavior is that, for example, your partner leaves you outside that stage and is with you for less and less time.

How do you get these specifics for information? Via the study of living together. Without transcending this reality at some stage, it is impossible to establish a parallel relationship over time.

Chat with your partner

Your mood and reaction will provide you with details about what is going on. Simply because in this moment of conflict you know your partner very well and their answer will make you see if you notice change or if, on the contrary, face the situation with the naturalness of always.

That does not indicate that he is remembered automatically by an unfaithful person. However, his verbal and body language, predisposition to speak about the subject, or whether he retains eye contact can be observed (a gesture that reflects sincerity).

What to do if I get cheated on by my boyfriend with another woman

The state of disbelief and shock is the first normal reaction for those who know that their partner is unfaithful. The state of confusion and frustration is apparent from a situation that breaks with previous standards, even though the data points in that direction. The person has the impression that he has witnessed a hoax.

Focus your attention on your partner, but not on the person who is outside the relationship. If you weigh the likelihood of a second chance or decisively close the door, analyze this reality about how it affects you both. How did you get here? What is the general equilibrium of the partnership before this case?

You can feel so many conflicting thoughts and ambivalent emotions when you are going through such a situation that putting them in writing can help you put that inner world in order.

The opinion you have about this scenario would be closely related to your own beliefs and the point of view you have about unfaithfulness. Some people view this reality as unforgivable; others think differently. When this fact has happened, continue to listen to your point of view, not only concerning what you have thought so far but also with what you think in the present.

What's it that your partner wants? This data is very significant, as there must be a shared disposition to create a new opportunity between them. You should allow yourself the opportunity to talk, explain thoughts or even do pair therapy. Forgiveness is the only true way to remedy infidelity. A complicated gesture that you can, therefore, respect. And you will know this only through the time that calms the emotions.

Context Analysis Infidelity is a composite of what occurred, but several other specifics are available. For instance, if your partner told you on his own initiative about infidelity or if you discovered it, or if it was a timely occurrence or a recurrent situation, or if you are in love with that person...

How do you gain immunity if your boyfriend cheats on you with another woman?
This reality places you in time in a complicated context. However, endless thoughts of the past come to your mind as you live in the present, and you wonder how this could happen to you. This scenario allows you not to ask yourself why it happened to you, but what you will do from now on. What is the distinction between the two questions?
The dilemma of 'why' interacts with searching for an objective purpose that you cannot always accomplish. There are many circumstances in life in which, while not having conclusive answers, we must continue going forward. Do you think if your partner gave you a reason for what happened, you would feel calmer? That would probably not change your mood at all.

If you concentrate on what you are going to do from now on, however, you do not eradicate the pain at once if you put yourself on a real plane in which you make decisions about what depends on you, but you do not position yourself in the role of a victim. You can't change the recent past, but you can write a page for today.

When infidelity occurs, it also happens that the person becomes aware of the details of the relationship to others who have not given too much meaning until then. That is, you can understand that it was not love that went through its best moment. However, infidelity creates this emotional storm that, as no event has done, shakes the foundations of the narrative.

And in such a sudden shift, finding comfort in you will allow you to be engaged in something that distracts you from your inner frustration by concentrating on certain plans or tasks that you want to do from now on. It is not about stopping the introspection that is so much needed but about realizing that life goes on.

CHAPTER FOUR

HOW TO RECOGNIZE A LOUSY COWORKER

"When climbing a mountain, nobody leaves a partner to reach the top alone."

-Tenzing Norgay-

(He and his partner Edmund Hillary were the first to crown Everest)

Perhaps you are a nuisance to your classmates and do not know. That is independent of how productive you are. We help you discover it by presenting some frequent habits of bad coworkers:

They impose their way of working
Except for requests made by a superior, which are a separate matter, we should not tell our peers how they should work. Each person is organized in a way. Indications such as "I prefer you pass it to me in an Excel" or "send me the invitation in a Google Calendar" can be intrusive. For example, if we prefer another file format, it is more considered that we are the ones who perform that conversion.
Likewise, instead of saying "call me when you read this" as an order, it is a good option to ask the other person how they prefer to work or present your suggestions without making them an order.

They save their own time by having others spend it
If they don't remember the date of an event, they write an email to someone who does know to ask it instead of doing a search in their inbox or online to find it. Or they ask questions to the whole team whose answer is with a simple Google search.

They also often ask someone to do a task instead just because that person takes less time to do it.

These people do their job well, but they do it at the cost of taking advantage of the time of others.

They don't put themselves in the place of the people they work with

It is common for the work of a person to start from what others did previously, or to pass to others who will work with him later. For that reason, it is important to put yourself in the shoes of the person who receives the part you have done: have you properly transmitted all the information you had? Have you been as advanced as you could? Is what you sent the best version of the work you can pass to your partner? The option that bad co-workers choose is to send their part "in any way", since their individual work will not stand out in the result.

They take previous knowledge for granted

For example, they send long chains of mails instead of making a summary that takes into account the data that the person has on that matter and makes him understand before and better. They do not consider that the time it would take to write that summary is very short compared to the time a person who does not know anything about the subject takes to understand a chain of e-mails read backward.

They love the "tailor's drawers," physical or digital

When transferring information to a partner, instead of unifying and ordering it, they resend everything in their hand. They do not organize or eliminate repetitions. They think that it is better to deliver "everything," so that they ensure that the recipient obtains it as it came to them, without considering how useful it can be to do a previous job of filtering and sorting.

They don't use email in a considerate way

The mistakes that are made when using email are numerous. Some of the most inconsiderate with the receiver is the following: including many people in a copy without explaining who they are or why they are there, abusing the "reply to all" button, addressing issues outside of what your subject announced in an email, responding partially instead of waiting to have the answer to everything to send a single email instead of several, etc.

They think that helping others is a waste of time
It bothers them to ask for help, they do so reluctantly. Whenever they can, they show the help they have provided, they throw it in their face or ask for something in return. They make it clear that they were participants in the result.
"I just do my job" is an ambiguous phrase. Doing the minimum required, without worrying about facilitating the work of others or providing extra help to the company, is an inconsiderate position.

They leave evidence to others
They have no qualms about ridiculing a partner if they get over that. They don't stop to consider that that is saying something even worse about them.

They put buts without offering solutions
They tend to say the negative of the work of others in an unconstructive way. They are not decisive. They launch their objections leaving the conversation open, without offering a solution or closing the argument. They are experts in leaving the discussions unfinished, either in person or by other means, rather than looking for effective ways to settle them.

They don't recognize their mistakes
Everyone is wrong at work at some point. The difference is in "throwing balls out" and blaming other partners or on the other hand taking responsibility and transmitting the purpose of amending the failures in the future. A person who does not try to sweep his mistakes under the carpet and who shows a real will to improve gives confidence and security to his superiors.

They are closed to changes
They like to use phrases like "that can't be done" or "we've never done it that way." They are anchored in a comfort zone and are not open to innovate and improve. They are skeptical of any proposed change that changes the routine they are used to.

According to some experts, it is preferable to hire empathic employees than professionals with extensive experience in the field.

In fact, the costs of dealing with a toxic person on the staff far outweigh the costs of hiring a worker with a higher salary, according to a study by Harvard University.

Therefore, in the long run, it will always be better hiring someone that creates a better working environment.

CO-WORKER HAS BECOME AN ENEMY

Many people around the world spend much of the day in the offices next to individuals outside the family environment: peers, who, over time, become a fundamental part of life.

Ideally, a relationship of friendship and solidarity is created where everyone supported and formed a work team capable of achieving the company's objectives.

However, sometimes this does not happen and that is when the office becomes a true battlefield where the opponents are attacked with subtle weapons and smiles that hide the rancor and the desire to annihilate.

Enemies have different characteristics and can be infiltrated anywhere in the organization chart. This battle does not escape even the newly hired, since there could be a partner who, for example, already has envy for his youth and / or academic preparation.

How to recognize the enemy?
In these cases, the most important thing is to know how to recognize the enemy, and identify their strategies to combat it. But before launching into the attack, it is important to ask yourself if you are really working with the enemy or if it only exists in the imagination.

This is because you cannot reach an office and immediately classify all coworkers as enemies without knowing them. To avoid judging unfairly, we must analyze several factors such as the following:

If a gesture, comment or criticism is being taken as a personal attack that was not specifically directed at someone in particular.

If direct aggression is due to an event that can justify the attitude of that person.

If the person who is assaulting is someone who used to treat everyone badly and does not have the purpose of destroying the professional development of any person.

Define the enemy
If after this analysis, it is concluded that the coworker does not have good intentions towards us, it would be necessary to define his characteristics, techniques of action and objectives to be able to counteract his attacks in a positive way. There are several types of enemy in an office that are classified as:

- **The aggressive**

Those who manifest their aggressiveness with direct attacks (screams, insults and even embarrassing scenes in public). In this case, it is best to remain calm and respond in a tone of dignity where professional boundaries are marked. In this way it is shown that he who has a real problem is the one who manifests his aggressiveness (since he does not know how to control it) and not you.

- **The hypocrite**

He may be smiling, but, from behind, he can speak ill of one and through gossip and scathing comments do us great harm in our image. In this case, the hypocrite must be confronted directly, without losing his smile (using his own technique), who will feel bad when unmasked, since he least wishes to be discovered.

- **The partner hand in hand**

He is located on the next table (usually doing the same functions as you) and is aware of any mistakes you make, highlights any defects you observe to comment or report it to the boss. This type of partner considers that the company is not large enough so that both can stay. Given this circumstance, you should strive in your performance, avoiding giving reasons to that enemy to talk about you and, at the same time, you should ignore it.

- **Those that are grouped with others**

Usually this type of enemy does not work alone but is grouped with others (his faithful friends) to make your life impossible with his indirect words oriented in most cases to your personal life (especially attacks in the cafeteria of the company at the time of lunch). It is possible to get rid of them using those who are mediators between one and the true aggressor.

Women don't work
Although we are in the nineteenth century, there are men who still consider that the place of women is the home and not the office and see them as rivals that must be fought and overcome (especially if the woman occupies an important position within the company and can scale to another above them). In this case, you should continue performing the functions as usual and keeping at bay any sexist comment that may be issued by them.

Here I am the boss
The worst enemy you can have is the boss. That battle has always been considered a loss, since at any time and for any excuse, they can do without your services. In this case, it is better, once this type of enemy is identified, to begin immediately to seek employment elsewhere.
Other partners who are not enemies, but who require special attention:

The lazy companion
Sometimes we meet colleagues who do not handle their workload well and ask for a favor or to help them to fulfill their assignments.

If the situation is repeated very often, care must be taken; They may want, deep down, for you to do their job while he or she is distracted or chatting with other colleagues. There are even those who, if something goes wrong, throw in your face the fact that you did not help him well.

Before the first symptom of this type of partner, you should not make personal attacks such as saying "you are a fresco". It is better to comment on the tone of constructive professional criticism. It is preferable to say something like "I can help you develop a system so that you can discover errors in time and organize your time better". It is important to make it clear that you will not carry their load but can teach them to "fish."

Peers who criticize labor issues
Sometimes we are the problem and it seems to us that our colleagues are giving us constant and unfounded criticism about some process of our work that we are not doing properly. Attitudes such as "treat as they treat you," "an eye for an eye," "a tooth for a tooth," or "If you criticize me, I criticize you," should be avoided, as it would be acting defensively and, perhaps worsening, the situation.

It is positive to do a self-analysis to evaluate if they could be right. Even, ask a colleague, whom you have the confidence or that you consider objective and fair, to indicate if there really is the problem for which they are criticizing you.

If he tells you that the criticism is founded, it is necessary to determine what actions to take to improve. At the same time, you should share relaxed moments with your colleagues so that they also perceive your attitude change. Sit with them at lunchtime or attend activities outside of work such as being part of the sports team.

What to avoid
There are attitudes that are fatal for anyone who wants to stand out in their profession when there are enemies in sight:

- **The fear of making decisions.** All who manage to climb have to dominate it, since the greater the authority, the greater the implied responsibilities. As recommended, act very firmly and objectively.

- **They do not know how to delegate responsibilities.** There are those who have the need to control everything, because they believe that no one can do better. This is a double fixed knife, since it wastes the person's time and reduces the creative capacity of others. In addition, it lowers the morale of the employees because they realize the lack of trust they have.
- **Not recognize the merits.** These individuals suffer a personality problem and compensate it by despising or ignoring the qualities of others. Therefore, they avoid giving public or private recognition. This attitude demoralizes and generates tension, which creates a very suitable environment to win enemies.

In conclusion, we must consider this situation as opportunities that help grow both emotionally and professionally, as they allow us to learn to deal with different personalities and conflicts. This can become a strength when it comes to professional success.

Remember never to take attitudes that generate even greater conflicts; that will only make the situation worse and work against you as it becomes part of the problem. It is not about winning a war or making it, but about finding harmony within differences.

CHAPTER FIVE

CHARACTERISTICS OR PROFILE OF AN ASSERTIVE AND NON-ASSERTIVE PERSON

The three different communication styles are passive, aggressive and assertive. The styles form a continuum, the passive and aggressive styles being the two extremes and the assertive style being the midpoint, that is, the optimum grade. Assertiveness is a way of communicating with others essential to have quality social relationships.

Assertiveness Characteristics

What is assertiveness? The definition of assertiveness consists of a set of practical social and communication skills. Assertive communication is based on respect for all parties and its objective is to negotiate an intermediate point between various positions. One of the most important characteristics of assertiveness and assertive attitude is the balance that it seeks and that contributes to communication. Its benefits are remarkable, as they allow improving communication and maintaining healthier and more satisfying relationships. It also helps strengthen self-esteem, since self-respect is a basic pillar for assertiveness.

The assertiveness and assertive attitude are to express one's opinion and defend a point of view or some ideas taking into account the rights themselves, but also those of others. Respecting the point of view of the other, assertiveness promotes understanding and empathy and allows us to reach a common point.

Characteristics of an assertive person

People's communication fluctuates in this continuum depending on situations and circumstances, but they have a general tendency towards a communicative style. For example, assertive people can sometimes adopt a characteristic attitude of passive or aggressive communication style. However, they are categorized in the assertive communication style because they show a general tendency to relate with assertiveness. With the following description and the list of features, you can easily identify an assertive person.

Assertive person: definition
What is an assertive person? The Assertive people are those who practice assertive communication style. Assertive behavior is based on respect for others and for oneself. Assertive people know their own rights and defend them, respecting others, that is, they will not "win", but "reach an agreement." They follow the method I win, you win.

Assertive person: characteristics
What are the characteristics of an assertive person? The qualities of an assertive person are the following:

- Speak calmly and directly. In an assertive person we can observe adequate fluidity, volume and speed, safety, direct eye contact, body relaxation, postural comfort and the absence of blockages or crutches. His facial expression is friendly and he smiles frequently. He pauses and silences. He says what he means directly. He knows how to make and receive compliments, and also asks and answers questions properly. His gestures are firm but not abrupt.
- Express your thoughts and opinions. The assertive person is able to express what he thinks, although his opinions differ from those of the rest. He can speak openly and honestly about his tastes and interests. He is able to express his disagreement with others and say "no."
- Respect the opinions of others. An assertive person knows how to accept their mistakes and knows how to respect the position of others, even if they do not share it.
- Express your feelings. Assertive people are able to express both positive and negative feelings.

- Considers everyone's rights. Assertive people know and believe in rights for themselves and for others. They defend their own respecting those of others. They do not get too close to their interlocutor, but respect their personal space.
- Acts adaptively. The assertive person adapts to the context and acts in the most effective way in each situation.
- Has healthy self-esteem. The assertive person does not feel inferior or superior to others, does not need to prove anything through aggressive communication. She feels good about herself and does not pretend to hurt others.
- They communicate from serenity. Another of the qualities of assertive people is that they speak from the calm and when the emotional intensity has decreased, producing the feeling of emotional control.
- Your goal is the midpoint. An assertive person is not interested in getting what he wants at any price, but rather to reach an agreement between the two parties and that both benefit.
- Has satisfactory and fruitful interpersonal relationships. Assertive people enjoy interpersonal relationships. Their way of communicating favors that they are well-valued by others and facilitates that they have a social support network.

Assertive person: examples
An example of a dialogue with an assertive person:

- Person 1: "Hello! Have you brought me the book I left you?"
- Person 2: "I have not brought it, I have forgotten again."
- Person 1: "I understand that you are busy with many things, but I need the book and many times you forget, what do you think if tomorrow I send you a message to remind you?"
- Person 2: "Perfect!"

Characteristics of a non-assertive person: passive communication

A non-assertive person is the one who has a tendency to an assertive communication style, that is, passive or aggressive. Next we will see in detail these communication styles.

Passive communication: characteristics

The characteristics of a passive person are as follows:
- Speak little and low. In a passive person we can observe that he speaks with a low volume of voice and in a little fluid way, he presents blockages, stutters, hesitations, and silences. People with a passive communication style use the words "maybe" and "I guess" a lot. They ask a few questions and answer with few words. They speak fast and unclear. They do not maintain eye contact, they have low eyes, tense faces, clenched teeth and trembling lips, nervous hands and tense and uncomfortable postures. They smile little and make nervous movements.
- He does not express his thoughts and opinions. The passive person is not able to express what he thinks, especially if his opinions differ from those of the rest.
- Put the opinions of others first. A passive person respects the opinions of others and puts them before their own. Thus they avoid disturbing or offending others. They are "sacrificed" people who live worried about satisfying others.
- He does not express his feelings. Passive people often feel misunderstood, manipulated and disregarded, but they do not manifest it. So they show emotional dishonesty. Although angry, they do not show anger or disagreement, they do not express their true feelings. In the following paragraph, you will find why it is so difficult to express feelings.
- Take into account the rights of others. Passive people put the rights of others before canceling their own. They respect others scrupulously but do not respect themselves.
- Act from fear. The passive person feels insecure and does not want to disturb others.

- He has low self-esteem. The passive person has low self-esteem, does not feel good about himself and therefore needs to be loved and appreciated by everyone. Consequently, he acts to please others.
- They hold others accountable. Passive people frequently complain about others: "X doesn't understand me," "Y is an egoist and takes advantage of me," and so on.
- His goal is not to get angry. A passive person is terrified of conflicts, does not know how to deal with disagreement with others and is unable to think about the possibility of facing someone. Therefore, he prioritizes the opinions and wishes of others at any price.
- He has insane interpersonal relationships. Passive people cannot enjoy social relationships. Maintaining this communicative style causes frequent feelings of anxiety, frustration, sadness and helplessness.

Passive communication: example
An example of habitual responses by a passive person is as follows:

- Person 1: "Hello! Have you brought me the book I left you?"
- Person 2: "I have not brought it, I have forgotten again."
- Person 1: "Well, nothing happens, it doesn't matter."
- Person 2: "It doesn't bother you, right?"
- Person 1: "Well, I needed it today, but it's the same."
- Person 2: "Well, I'll bring it to you tomorrow, okay?"
- Person 1: "Okay."

Characteristics of a non-assertive person: aggressive communication
Non-assertive people are those who tend to behave passively or aggressively. The aggressive communication style is the opposite of the passive, it is the other end of the continuum. At both ends, the ideal would be to work social skills to get closer to the center.

Aggressive communication: features
The characteristics of an aggressive person are the following:

- Talk a lot and loud. In an aggressive person we can observe that he speaks with a high volume of voice, fast and emphatically. He uses imperative and derogatory language with foul words and even insults and threats. Throws many linked questions and answers quickly. A challenging attitude is perceived in eye contact. He usually shows his face and tense hands and adopts a body posture that invades the personal space of the interlocutor, so that he feels invaded and intimidated. Gestures with threatening movements.

- **Express your thoughts and opinions without the filter.** The aggressive person expresses what he thinks and believes without taking into account the feelings of others.

- **Put your opinions and wishes first.** An aggressive person expresses their wishes and opinions as the only valid options. He does not respect the opinions of others. Sometimes, he doesn't even allow them to express them.

- **Express your emotions uncontrollably.** Aggressive people often have sudden excessive outbursts of aggression. These outbursts are usually quite uncontrolled, as they are the result of an accumulation of tensions and hostility. He lacks social skills to regulate his expression.

- **He does not take into account the rights of others.** Aggressive people defend their interests without respecting the rights of others.

- **Act from fear.** The aggressive person thinks that if they do not behave in this way, they are excessively vulnerable.

- **He has low self-esteem.** The aggressive person does not feel good about themselves and therefore needs to be respected by others, defend themselves by attacking and "win" the other in communication.

- **Does not listen.** The aggressive person communicates unidirectionally, does not listen and has an attitude of contempt for others.

- **Your goal is to win.** An aggressive person cannot stand that things do not go as he wants. He thinks that the important thing is to get what he wants at any price.
- **He has insane interpersonal relationships.** It is complicated to deal with aggressive people and cause rejection in others. So they may feel lonely, frustrated, misunderstood and guilty. Their attitude of contempt and disrespect can generate great conflicts in their interpersonal relationships.

Aggressive communication: example

An example of a dialogue with an aggressive person is as follows:

- Person 1: "Hello! Have you brought the book I left you?"
- Person 2: "I didn't bring it, I forgot it again."
- Person 1: "But it's the fourth time you forget it!"
- Person 2: "I was going to take it, but in the end I forgot."
- Person 1: "It's always the same, you don't remember anything. I want it right now."

HOW TO LEARN TO BE ASSERTIVE

How to learn to be assertive with positive communication? Assertive communication opens doors in your life, since, through this experience, you have the ability to express your opinions and points of view while respecting your rights, but also those of those around you. There is an interpersonal relationship scheme that can help you to walk in the direction of assertiveness: "I am fine, you are fine." That is, position yourself in a framework of reality in which two people relate from interpersonal equality.

Express your opinions to be assertive

You are a unique and unrepeatable person. You can bring your own essence to others. Therefore, value your own voice and your views. It is not about imposing your opinions, but expressing them naturally. Sometimes people avoid showing their opinions for fear of conflict.

If you have ever felt this way, then start taking the initiative to show your opinions in simple and concrete actions. For example, if you have been to the movies with your group of friends, express clearly which movies you are especially interested in and which ones you don't want to watch.

Learn to say no to gain assertiveness

How many times do you suffer from your own internal contradictions by saying yes to something you really wanted to say no to? "No" is a short word, however, it produces such a psychological impact on the mind of the person who pronounces this message that, when a person has a low level of assertiveness, he suffers when setting limits.

Remember that when you say no to someone else's request, you are not rejecting that someone, you are simply putting into practice your ability to decide. Stop justifying yourself for everything as if you really had to. The language is rich and broad. Therefore, use it to open doors.

How to learn to be assertive in practice?

Imagine that a friend wants to talk to you today to tell you about an important issue, but you had a horrible day and you don't have a good disposition to really focus on that conversation. In that case, you can express an assertive message of this type: "Thank you very much for sharing with me what has happened to you. Today I had a bad day and I am very tired. If you think so, we can talk tomorrow. Then, I can spend time with you and give you the attention you deserve."

Too often, we move in a narrow frame of closed questions that only admit the answer of "yes" or "no". However, it is important that you make positive use of the language to use it in its full range of nuances.

Defend your rights

Another secret to being more assertive is to express the messages in the first person. For example, imagine that you often get angry at a friend because he arrives late for the plans and you always have to wait. In that case, a frequent mistake is to fall into reproach through messages such as "you are unpunctual."

To gain assertiveness, try to express your requests following the essence of the "I". For example, you can express this idea: "When you're late for our plans, I feel you don't value my time and that makes me feel sad." When we express an idea in the first person we awaken more empathy in the other. That is, assertiveness invites understanding.

Although language opens doors when used correctly, remember that you don't just express a message through the word. It is important that your tone of voice is also aligned with the verbal message and body language information. Currently, there are many different means of communication. However, if you have to address an important issue, it is better to talk with that person face to face, since eye contact creates a climate of emotional confidence.

Assertive Words

Another of the best techniques to be assertive is to take care of your communication: "Thank you", "I'm sorry", "I love you" and "please". Beautiful, simple and constructive words that, used in the right context, are a clear example of assertiveness. That is, do not hesitate to apologize if you were wrong. Appreciate the beautiful gestures that other people have with you in the daily routine.

Express your feelings of affection with freedom and naturalness. At work, remember that the formula "please" generates empathy and kindness. Language builds your reality. Therefore, try to make your words positive and kind.

CHAPTER SIX

COMMUNICATION LEVELS: VERBAL, PARA-VERBAL, NON-VERBAL

When we communicate, we send a lot more of what we want to say with our words: the gestures, posture, tone of voice, even silence can reveal emotions and thoughts, influencing the effectiveness of our message.

There are three levels of communication: verbal, para-verbal and non-verbal. The difference between those who know how to communicate effectively and those who, on the other hand, fail to convey the message in the desired way lies in the ability to fine-tune these levels.

How you do it? First of all, you need to know all the levels well and know how to manage them simultaneously.

The three levels of communication

Verbal communication
Verbal communication is made up of the words we use when we speak or write, and it usually is also the level of which we are most aware, the one we treat most carefully.

When we have to express ourselves, in fact, we try to choose words carefully, adapting the register to our interlocutor: if we are in a formal context, we will use a more sophisticated language; if we talk in an informal setting, we will use a more colloquial jargon. In general, we try to construct the discourse in a way that is clear and understandable, as well as persuasive, and to arouse interest and curiosity in the interlocutor.

Paraverbal communication
The second level of communication is the paraverbal one, or the way we say something.

In oral communication, the indicators are the tone, speed, timbre, and volume of the voice. In the case of written communication, we have, for example, the punctuation and the length of the periods, elements that give the text rhythm and speed.

Compared to the first level, we are less aware of these aspects. If, in fact, it is reasonable to prepare a speech or choose some words instead of others, it is less usual to decide the tone of voice or the timbre. Communication professionals do it, while "non-experts" use Para verbal communication in a natural way, without paying particular attention to it.

Non-verbal communication
The third level concerns the non-verbal, which is all that is transmitted through one's posture, one's movements, the position occupied in space with respect to the interlocutor, but also one's own way of dressing.

The non-verbal language is also present when we communicate in writing: if we write by hand, the calligraphy or type of card used can reveal our mood or the care we have in writing the message; in an email, the type of font, the color, the possible use of images are essential indicators.

Even in this case, we are not always aware of how these elements reveal something about us and, vice versa, how important it is to know how to read them to understand better who is facing us.

MICROEXPRESSIONS THAT GIVE YOU AWAY

Small expressions are very fast and unintentional expressions that occur as manifestations of the emotions we feel. I will tell you the secrets: these can tell you what the person we are interacting with is feeling.

Learning to identify them promotes your personal relationship by improving your emotional expression thereby improving the emotional expression of your partner, friends, family, etc.

With this trick, you can understand that you can experience the desired emotional response by manipulating the body language. In other words, we have an incredible power that creates emotion through expression.

> *"The most important thing in communication is knowing how to listen to what is not said."*
>
> *- Peter Drucker -*

Paul Ekman, the maximum exponent of microexpressions, affirms that they are biological expressions and not learned. So it is a universal aspect of the human being.

HOW MANY FACIAL EXPRESSIONS DO WE HAVE?

To date, over 10,000 different facial expressions have been cataloged, and only seven basic facial expressions have been identified. A microexpression is a universal and subtle gesture that allows us to read the emotions of the face of the person we are looking at and constitutes the basis for the rest of the facial expression.

The 7 basic microexpressions are constituted by the following:

1. **Anger**
   The microexpression of anger is mainly concentrated in the upper part of the face, where we lower and join the eyebrows with a frown. We usually squeeze and tighten the mouth, slightly separating the lips and clenching the teeth. The look is penetrating.

An own gesture of anger consists in pointing with the chin forward in a defiant way.

2. **Fear**
   This subtle expression feels dangerous somewhere, and is characterized by strained eyebrows and large eyes to visualize everything we can do from our vision.
   At the bottom of the face, the jaws loosen and the lips stretch slightly. This constitutes an instinctive action to scream and take in oxygen. In this way, the mouth is slightly half open.

3. **Joy**
   Joy is shown with diagonal eyes and wrinkles on the outer edge and lower eyelid. Secret: When a person pretends to be joyful, those wrinkles are not formed. It also shows a characteristic smile.

4. **Light emptiness**
   In this expression, the upper part of the face can adopt various gestures, and the lower part of the face can find a key to identify it.

5. **The surprise**
   It is characterized by raised and arched eyebrows with wide eyes. In the lower part of the face the jaw is loose and the mouth is open.
   «In a conversation, body language is much more important than verbal and through body language there is a lot of information that we don't say and we rarely observe».

6. **Sorrow**
   This is one of the most complicated micro-expressions to pretend. It is characterized by low eyebrows that meet delicately in the center. The corners of the lips tend to go down and can even show tremors.

"Most lies are successful because no one wants to know the truth."

-Paul Ekman-

7. Disgust

This microexpression is one of the most easily identifiable because all expressions are concentrated between the mouth and nose. The nose is wrinkled, the upper lip is raised, and often the upper teeth are not visible. While the lower eyelid is wrinkled, wrinkles also occur around the nose and forehead, as well as cheek bulges.

But we don't just show that when we try to eat something that causes disgust. It also shows in a personal relationship when you feel disapproved or hate someone. Disgust is an emotion that can be translated into ideological rejection, as opposed to our ideology. So, for example, observing this expression in a discussion is not strange.

CHAPTER SEVEN

BEHAVIOR, DEVIANT BEHAVIOR AND PSYCHOLOGY

Behavioral psychology is a field of knowledge that explains the nonverbal movements of the body (facial expression, gestures, intonations) of a person and draws conclusions about how sincere, true, confident and open a person is.

Very often we make such an assessment unconsciously when we feel uncomfortable when we are communicating with, or even avoiding, a familiar person. But we actually appreciate his behavioral manifestations, which tell us what he thinks of us, how he relates, despite the fact that his words may be sympathetic or neutral.
There are a number of techniques for determining a person's true intentions, his emotions, and his level of self-esteem. His movements, facial expressions, and other features reveal his inner fears, attitudes, complexes that we perceive unknowingly or consciously if we have some knowledge and experience.

We perceive the process of communication as a general picture, sometimes during a conversation, we do not notice what we are wearing, what we say, but we pay attention to how we do it, what phrases and words we use, how we sit and what we hold in our hands. Sometimes little things get attention and are remembered for a long time: smell, speech difficulty, accent, reservations, wrong accents, inappropriate giggles, etc.

The scientific discipline that helps to explain and decipher the unconscious nuances in the behavior of people who give their true intentions is the psychology of behavior.

1. **What do gestures and facial expressions tell us?**
   Facial gestures and expressions play a huge role in the conversation. But despite the simplicity of decoding a person's postures and gestures, they can have a completely different meaning.

For example, in the psychology of lies, there are basic signs of deception: one does not look into his eyes, touch the mouth, nose, neck. But the other person can also touch his nose because of itching.

Crossed legs or arms - these gestures in the psychology of human behavior are interpreted as distrust, tightness, isolation, but the interlocutor may just be cold.

Tips for deciphering manners and gestures can often lead to a dead-end or confuse a person. For example, after seeing the interviewee's open position, confident and calm voice, the pleasant honest look, we consider him an honest man when in fact, he has deceptive intentions. Or pickups, how much charm, wit, sincerity, good breeding they have - and that's all they need to establish themselves.

2. What do speech and intonation tell us?
Speech speed, rhythm, volume, and intonation greatly influence communication and can tell a great deal more information about a person, as behavior psychology considers. Science helps to understand a person's emotional state:

- A calm, sensible, balanced person speaks rhythmically, slowly, with a moderate level of loudness.
- The impulsive character gives a quick and lively speech.
- Those who are not confident or closed-minded speak softly, hesitantly.

3. Often words are not as important as intonation
But it must be understood that if a person is in an unfamiliar environment, he may behave differently than in a familiar environment.
The psychology of behavior will allow you to identify the hidden factors that actually affect a person. But in order to see and understand them, we need to be "grounded" through knowledge and attentive to people.

DEVIANT BEHAVIOR AND PSYCHOLOGY

The phenomenon of such behavior is so complex and widespread that, in order to study it, there is a separate science - deviant theory, which emerged at the intersection of criminology, sociology, psychology, and psychiatry.

1. **The concept of "deviant" and social behavior in psychology**

"Deviation" from Latin - "Deviation". In psychology, deviant behavior from accepted norms in society is called deviant or asocial. It is a sustainable human behavior that causes real harm to people and society. This is harmful to others as well as to the deviant itself.

The psychology of deviant behavior explores such forms of deviation as suicide, crime, prostitution, drug addiction, wandering, fanaticism, alcoholism, and vandalism.

Such behavior is related to anger, violence, aggression, and destruction, therefore the society has conditionally or lawfully imposed penalties on the offender of social norms; he is isolated, treated, corrected or punished.

2. **The identity of the deviant, his psychology, behavior**

Science does not study how and where a person has committed a crime; it is interested in common patterns and personality traits.

Causes and sources of asocial behavior:

- **Physiological:** Genetic predisposition to aggression; endocrine diseases; chromosomal abnormalities.
- **Public:** Imperfect legislation; social inequality; promoting anti-social lifestyle in the media; hangs "labels"; negative evaluations they give to local people.

- **Psychological causes:** Internal conflicts between conscience and desires; special character of the character; mental anomalies; dysfunctional family relationships; too conservative, rigorous, cruel upbringing in childhood.

In the nature of deviations, characteristics such as conflict, negativism, dependence, anxiety, aggression, and hostility are common. They often cheat and do it with pleasure, they like to transfer responsibility and blame to others.

A person's deviant behavior leads to social maladaptation, i.e., he does not adapt to the conditions of society and, as a result, opposes it.

The child's behavior cannot be asocial as children under the age of 5 have not yet developed self-control and the process of adaptation in society has just begun.

The most dangerous period in terms of the possibility of deviation is between the ages of 12 and 20 years.

3. How to deal with behavior problems?
Most often people with such behavior go to a psychologist already in detention centers, in children's colonies, in addiction treatment centers. The society deals with the prevention of deviations in hospitals, schools, the media, but the problem is that there is no individual approach and one cannot handle it alone. But he may realize the need to change his lifestyle and seek the help of specialists.

PSYCHOLOGY OF ADDICTIVE BEHAVIOR

In psychology, addiction is called the science of human behavior, attachment to someone or something. It is unacceptable from the point of view of moral or social norms, endangering the health and causing suffering to the person.

Addiction harms society and humans, limits one's development and leads to all kinds of mental illness.

More people die from addiction than crime and war together. It manifests itself as an escape from problems in an illusory ideal world. Gradually the person ceases to control his behavior, emotions, and thoughts. His entire existence is reduced to the object of dependence, which gradually completely destroys him as a human being.

The widespread use of drugs and alcohol among young people has recently become a national disaster. That is why the attention of psychologists, psychiatrists, sociologists, drug addicts, and lawyers is directed at this issue.

Addictive behavior is also called addiction-this is a kind of deviant behavior. That is, the desire to escape from reality by changing your mental consciousness. Behavioral psychology sees this as a destructive attitude towards the self and society. Addictive behavior includes alcoholism, drug addiction, smoking, increased libido, gambling, computer addiction, abundant food poisoning, and shopping.

Addiction has different weights, from normal to severe.

Why do some people form this strong and attractive attachment that explains the impulsiveness and frustration of attraction? The answers to these questions are most important for society and all individuals.

PSYCHOLOGY OF GESTURES AND FACIAL EXPRESSIONS

The psychology of behavior, gestures and facial expressions are the keys to the secrets the person wants to hide. As a result of evolution, man has learned to convey thoughts and feelings through words. But with this skill, he has mastered the art of hiding his true intentions and aspirations. You should be able to "read" your interlocutor in his gestures. Only in this way can one understand what is in his mind and what can be expected from him.

American psychologist Meyerabian Albert believes that when we communicate, we transmit 7% of the information verbally, 38% in intonation and tone of voice, 55% in non-verbal signals.

The basic rule of the psychology of gestures and facial expression is that there is no person in the world who can fully control the body's movements in the process of conversation, even if he wants to deliberately mislead the interlocutor.

A person at the subconscious level responds almost equally to certain situations. Forced facial expressions and gestures of a stranger allow you to hear and see the words hidden behind the screen.

- **Protection.** In dangerous or uncomfortable situations, when one wants to isolate himself from the other party - people lean back, close with a book, folder or another object, cross their legs, cross their arms over their breasts, or clench their fists. Their eyes are closely watched by those who expect the trick. Such behavior is alert and tense and does not require constructive dialogue.
- **Openness.** The body is inclined towards the interlocutor, open palms, benign smile - these signals indicate a predisposition to communication.
- **Interest.** Lack of gestures, talking about enthusiasm, a person full of attention, he leans forward and tries not to move so he doesn't miss a word.

- **Boredom.** Gone is the sight, the rhythmic shaking of his feet, something in his hands, attraction, yawning. In sign language in the psychology of communication, this means that the listener has no interest in the topic of the conversation.
- **Skeptical.** The man agrees with the interlocutor but makes it clear that he does not trust through such gestures as rubbing the neck, scratching his ear, cheek, forehead, smiling, or stuffing his chin with his palm.

The psychology of human behavior teaches us to understand the wisdom of non-verbal symbolism and the proper understanding of one another.

WHAT CAN A NONVERBAL WORD SAY ABOUT A PERSON?

Most people underestimate the role of facial expression and gestures in communication. But with the help of non-verbal signals, the first impression on the person is created. And he remembers it for a long time. The gestures help or distract the listeners from the conversation, even if the lack of it brings information about the person speaking.

So, what do these or other gestures mean:
- The slow handshake speaks of a person's shyness and insecurity, and vice versa - a strong desire to impose his or her opinion.
- If a woman fixes her hair, it means that she moves.
- If one gestures with one hand only, it shows his unnaturalness.
- Touching the forehead, mouth, nose is considered fraud.
- The crossing of arms speaks of skepticism and distrust of the interlocutor to the speaker.
- Bent down, hunched over, shows low self-esteem and insecurity.

It is necessary to develop the observation in itself, it helps to gather additional information about the people with whom the person should communicate.

Essential in the psychology of human behavior is the ability to listen and see. After all, the sound of the voice and its intonation, gestures and facial expressions of the interlocutor are of great importance.

WHAT DOES MALE BEHAVIOR TELL US
The strong half of humanity's psychology is always about performing certain actions. Conquer, win, and conquer. Therefore, in their childhood games, there is always a spirit of endurance, character, strength, and competition.

All actions are aimed at the final result. Their self-esteem since childhood is based on ability and achievement.

The words and actions of men and women are different. Therefore, when talking to them, you need to pay attention to the overall behavior. If he sits half-turned with his legs and an arm crossed during a conversation and does not listen, he will somehow block the information. When he looks into his eyes and sometimes sees his lips, he is passionate about conversation.

When a man straightens his tie, changes his posture, raises his eyebrows, or opens his eyes-he is interested in the woman who is talking.

If he avoids searching, pulling buttons, or other small details of clothing, covering his mouth with his hand and not keeping his shirt collar straight, the interviewee is trying to hide something.
Note that all these non-verbal signals are average. Strong sex psychology is much more complex and depends on the person and his emotional fullness.

WHAT DO OUR KIDS SAY ABOUT THEIR CRAZINESS?

The psychology of child behavior is based on three basic principles:

- A sense of belonging to the family system.
- Emotional relationships with parents.
- Self-importance.

When the child's basic needs are met (sleep, food, water), he or she is eager to satisfy the emotional ones. He should have some duties assigned to him alone. This is something that depends only on him. This increases his confidence. He must feel that he is contributing to the life of the family in order to know that his opinion is considered and that he also controls events.

How can we help the child and satisfy his or her need for relevance and commitment?

First of all, it is necessary to form a close emotional connection with mom, dad, and other relatives. And involve the child in discussing family problems, making decisions.

If there is a conflict with the child, talk to them, they may lack parental attention. He needs to make him understand that he is very important and necessary.

They spend time with the child for at least 20 minutes a day, but they should be devoted to it. Children love to make mistakes and play with their parents, thus establishing the strongest emotional connection. Do not teach him how to play with these or other toys, it is better to remain without judgment. He must have a sphere of life in which he alone must make decisions. Try to become a friend, not a caregiver.

PSYCHOLOGY OF WOMEN

The psychology of the beautiful half of humanity is based on several circumstances:
- The nature of the warehouse - Most women are optimistic. They are active, they are characterized by changes in mood, they are able to control the feelings and subordinate circumstances of their desires.
- Education - What parents put in a little girl determines her actions and behavior.

- Experience - If she has been confronted with
  negativity throughout her life, she stops believing in
  people and becomes lonely. Her behavior is different
  from the standard.

The psychology of a woman's behavior is determined by her
attitude towards the man. Psychologists believe that women
have natural resourcefulness that helps them in their lives. But
they focus their ingenuity on relationships with men. For
example, they try to look strong and independent, always have
hobbies, often plan personal time and so on.

FORMS OF HUMAN BEHAVIOR

- The behavior of leaders and practitioners is
  dominant.
- Creative - is characteristic of people with abstract
  thinking. They rely more on intuition, have ingenuity,
  foreboding, fantasy, completely detached from
  reality.
- The harmonizing behavior is characteristic of people
  who are endowed with empathy, ethics and subtle
  diplomacy.
- Normalization is the behavior of people with logic
  who are able to analyze facts.
- People usually combine two types of behavior, one of
  which is more pronounced.

HUMAN SOCIAL BEHAVIOR

It is an act or combination of them between and in relation to
people. At the same time, such actions must be socially
relevant - important to others.
Social behavior can be deviant and criminal (injurious to
others), adequate or inadequate to the situation and prevailing
circumstances, contradictory and conformal, etc.

Intentional and unintentional behavior is of great importance
in everyday communication and interaction. If a person has
performed a certain act without malicious intent, it does not
absolve him of responsibility, but to some extent mitigates the
sentence. And if behavior serves as a response (for example, a
provocation to conflict), responsibility is somewhat reduced.

Other equally important varieties are conscious and unconscious behavior. Although they are easily mistaken for deliberate and unintentional, these are different concepts. Unconscious behavior is an act whose motive and performance is not recognized by man. As a rule, it goes unnoticed by the most active but is well treated by others.

Human behavior is, for the most part, the social aspect, but it is also individual - it is carried out in the paradigm "I and objects". It is also classified as false and correct, adequate and inadequate, etc.

Other classification
According to other parameters, behavior is categorized as follows:

- Congenital
- Acquisition
- Creative

In the first case, the action is genetically programmed as an action. They include people who have learned in the first few hours of life.
In the second case, the behavior is formed as a result of training and education. There are many contradictions here. Detailed analysis of many behaviors clearly shows that they are genetically programmed, and training is just one type of catalyst for maturing the will to engage with them.

Some of the behaviors learned are also utterances, vocabulary norms, behavioral rules, basics, attitudes, etc. Another category is learning behavior-behavioral patterns formed by other important adult examples. In some cases, fear responses are addressed, such as when a child is not tall but has acrophobia.

Creative action-action created by a person himself. This is a constructive and creative act.

There are many factors that affect human behavior, which is the most controversial issue in behavioral psychology. Currently, there are some basic concepts that describe human behavior.

1. **The theory of personality traits.** According to this guideline, human behavior is defined (predetermined) by individual traits. According to some researchers, a person may have 2 to 10 basic character traits that determine the overall "course" of his actions.
2. **The behaviorist theory.** It defines a behavioral act in response to a stimulus. Behavior is a set of emotional, motor, and speech reactions that are formed in response to the influence of the external environment.

   At birth, one already has a certain repertoire of genetic responses. In the course of life, the effect of the stimulus causes the creation of new reactions on the basis of this repertoire; the unconditional stimuli are combined with the conditional stimuli forming complex systems.
3. **The second theory created the theory of social learning.** According to this, human behavior is determined by roles and models. They, in turn, form in the process of observing social models. Personality is a product of the interaction between the self and the environment, so the behavior is influenced by the human environment, significant adults, film characters, teachers, comrades, and more. This theory explains well the variability of behavioral acts, depending on the circumstances, but pays little attention to personal qualities as a factor in determining behavioral patterns.
4. **Psychoanalytic theory.** It is the biggest antithesis to behaviorism and states that the behavior is the result of resolving the personal conflict. It arises between the three structures of the psyche: ID (This is the subconscious, instinct), Ego (I, the person) and Super Ego (the public, conscience, norms, principles). The leading role is played by ID, it is the one that drives the action, and behavior is defined as a set of behavioral actions in response to impulses of the ID. Uncoordinated aspirations are unconscious, so they must be recognized as internal conflicts and analyzed accordingly.

5. **Cognitive theory.** According to this theory, behavior is not a mechanical response to a stimulus, but the result of interpreting a particular situation, which is realized because of already existing knowledge and experience. Behavioral actions depend, first and foremost, on the person's own assessment of the circumstances, and therefore the objects of study should be: information acquisition, explanation, creation, and recognition of an image, imagination, speech, etc.

6. **Gestalt.** According to this theory, man perceives the world in the form of complete images, while interacting with the surrounding reality, he identifies the most important here and now the whole. Behavior is a manifestation of the form of an image. Therefore, the characterization of the here and now is fundamental in the interpretation of certain human actions.

7. **The theory of group dynamics.** Human behavior is directly dependent on collective activity, as not only the participation of the group but also its product. This assumption only works in terms of group behavior, more often in the work team.
A separate category of theories is sociological as they distribute a large enough number of them. They also view the behavior of the individual exclusively within a group or society.

Sociological theories

- **Typicality theory.** Behavior is determined by the presence of typical attributes, which in turn are formed by belonging to a category (cultural, national, professional, etc.).
- **The theory of social action.** Behavior is the result of actions that take into account the interests, needs, and perceptions of other participants.
- **Institutional.** Behavior is the role learned by the individual, namely the conformity of the actions within her framework with the norms.
- **Functional.** Behavior is the performance of a function established for the normal operation of the group.

- **Interactionism.** Behavior is the interaction between members of structural units, small groups within a large one.
- **Social conflict theory.** The behavior is a consequence of the clash of interests of the group members, as well as the social positions and opinions.
- **The theory of social exchange.** The basis of behavior is a rational, mutually beneficial exchange of benefits, activities, and rewards for them.
- **Phenomenological approach.** The basic aspect of this theory is the concept of the world of everyday life. He shares with many people in the process of life but does not exclude private, biographical points. There are personal or impersonal relationships in the world, and this determines human behavior.

CHAPTER EIGHT

RELATIONSHIPS BETWEEN EMOTIONS AND BEHAVIOR

Our behavior is the result of mutual cognitive interaction of rational and emotional abilities. The most primitive emotions (primary emotions) have a great influence on behavior.

However, some control over them is possible, but it requires special conditions (training, strong cultural and rational conditioning, etc.) and, even then, sometimes it is not possible to control them individually, needing the help of specialists (psychologist, psychiatrist, therapist in general).

A clear example is a fear, known and experienced by all and not always surpassed. In this case, even the full action of self-consciousness and experience may not be enough to overcome their innate actions (flight or paralysis) and to conduct a behavior more in line with rational processing of the situation.

Having countless situations in which emotions have a significant role, I wanted to expose only four cognitive and behavioral components related to emotions and with special importance in the development of our behavior.

Empathy. Emotions have a close relationship with the social production of empathy, whose definition would be to perceive in a common context what a different individual can feel. Empathy being strongly related to various brain structures can mirror neurons (prefrontal cortex and temporal) and without them (amygdala, and various structures of the limbic system). In empathy, three aspects can be distinguished:

- First, to know the feelings of another person, so it would be closely related to the Theory of the Mind (the cognitive component) and, therefore, with the development of self-awareness.
- Second, feel what the other is feeling, either similarly or equal to what the subject may feel in the same situation (emotional component).

- Third, respond compassionately to the problems that afflict you (social behavior).

Empathy seems to have a very important social role, which favors the development of social relations and social and personal consciousness. It exists in those behaviors that for its realization require reinforcements of social structures (migrations, social organization, distribution of work, etc.). According to various authors, it is essential for the development of ethical or moral behaviors.

Behavioral control. We can develop some control of the behavioral manifestation of emotions. This control can vary from a simple inhibition leaving the expression of emotions totally free, to elaborate gradual forms of limitation or voluntary variation of such manifestations.

In the second case, it would be closely related to the evolution of self-consciousness. Its existence or absence would facilitate extreme behaviors marked by behavioral denial, deception, lies, and violence, where empathy would be totally abolished. This cognitive function would be closely related to the executive functions of LPF (inhibition).

Motivation. Emotions condition the development of motivation to a great degree, and this is the main driver of behavior. It can be considered as the knowledge (by sensitive and/or rational) of the existence of facts that stimulate the need or interest (affective component, fundamental in human behavior) to develop better and more complex behaviors of all kinds (technological, social and symbolic) to reach a solution (goal).

The way we feel emotionally in a given situation is one of the most important elements of motivation. Technological, social and symbolic advances are responses to emotions that have motivated behaviors aimed at their resolution.

The influence of self-awareness on emotions. It would be conditioned to its own creation and evolution, which did not happen until the neuroevolution, socio-economic, demographic, technological and linguistic circumstances made it possible.

Its development is a heterogeneous continuum in time and space, so there are numerous intermediate stages in its progress throughout human evolution. Its action would produce modifications in all emotions (primary and secondary). Of the primary ones, control can only be given by joining the mechanisms of behavioral inhibition, from the secondary ones there can be large modulations giving rise to higher self-conscious or cognitive emotions.

CHAPTER NINE

BODY LANGUAGE

Body language is the subject of many studies and is the origin of many myths, such as what says 93% of communication is non-verbal.

Many people who read it have become popular because they are devoted to repeating it, but the real research that started that belief presents too many flaws to take up in the letter.

Nonetheless the impact of body language on our social skills is not negligible, in addition to being an excellent mirror of the real feelings of our interlocutors.
Certainly, you meet people who are distrusted, especially if they are not unpleasant or unfriendly. You couldn't say what it was specifically, but they give off an aura that they don't want to confess their true feelings.

That's because there is a discrepancy between their verbal communication and their body language, as this study demonstrated at the time.

On the other hand, other people give off a great charisma without any particular chat. Their physical expression is in harmony with their language and conveys confidence and warmth.

What is body language?
Body language is a form of communication that uses body and facial gestures, postures, and movements to convey information about the issuer's emotions and thoughts. Usually done at an unconscious level, it is usually a very clear indicator of people's emotional state. Along with voice inflection, it is part of nonverbal communication.

The body language should not be regarded as absolute truth. There are many environmental factors that can affect the language of the body. That is why the conclusion of interpreting a single body symbol should never be reached. What is important is to observe a set of matching signs and eliminate possible external causes (temperature, noise, fatigue, etc.).

That said; let's look at everything we can communicate with the body and face.

Key to body language
    1.   *The meaning of facial gestures*
Since the face is a magnifier of emotion, it is said to be a reflection of the soul. However, as with nonverbal language interpretations, facial gestures are usually part of a global emotional state and can cause different interpretations, so be careful not to evaluate facial gestures individually.

Isn't it true that when a child sees what he dislikes, he covers his eyes so that it disappears from reality? Or doesn't he run to cover his mouth after he lies?
Now, for adults, the size is much smaller, but to some extent, we are still connected to this primitive behavior. And it gives a lot of clues. Because we can still detect in our face unconscious attempts to block what we say, hear and see.

In general, when someone puts their hand on their face, it is usually the product of negative thoughts such as anxiety and distrust. Here are some specific examples:
- **Covering or touching the mouth:** If done while speaking, means trying to hide something. If it is done while listening, it may be a signal that the person believes something is hidden.
- **Touch the ear:** An unconscious expression of the desire to block audible words. If your talker does it while you are talking, it means he wants you to stop talking to you.
- **Touching the nose:** It may indicate that someone is lying. If you lie, catecholamines are released. Catecholamines can irritate the internal tissues of the nose and cause itching. It also happens when someone gets angry or worried.

- **Scratch one eye:** An attempt to block what you see so you don't have to face someone lying. When talking to you, beware of people who frequently touch the nose and rub their eyes.
- **Scratch your neck:** A sign of uncertainty or doubt about what you are saying.
- **Bring your finger or something in your mouth:** It means anxiety or you need to calm down with an unconscious expression of returning to the mother's safety.

2. *Head position*

Understanding the meaning of the various positions that the head can take is very effective in understanding their true intentions such as likes, cooperation, and rog pride.

Pay special attention to a very exaggerated posture. Because they do it consciously to influence you.

- **Raise your head and project your chin forward.** This is a sign that aims to express positiveness and power clearly.
- **To nod:** It is a contagious obedience gesture that can convey positive feelings. It conveys interest and consent, but if it is done very quickly several times, it can tell you that you have already heard a lot.
- **Tilt your head:** It is a sign of obedience by exposing your throat. Doing it while you're listening to someone's story shows your confidence in the talker. It has also been observed for women to be used to show interest in men.
- **Support your face with your hands.** Usually, the face is exposed to "present" to the interlocutor. Therefore, it shows appeal to others.
- **Put the chin in hand:** If the palm is closed, it is an evaluation signal. If your palm is open, it can mean boredom or loss of interest.

3. *It also talks about the appearance*

Communication through the line of sight is largely related to the dilation or contraction of the pupil in response to the internal conditions we experience. That is why bright eyes are more attractive than dark eyes. Bright eyes can more clearly show pupil enlargement, a reaction associated with positive emotions.

When speaking, you usually maintain eye contact for 40-60% of the time. That's because your brain is busy trying to access the information (NLP assumes that depending on the type of information you are trying to get, you are looking sideways, but it has already been shown that this is not true).

In certain social situations, the lack of eye contact can be interpreted as tension or embarrassment, so the time required to access information without having to look away simply by pausing before responding can be obtained.

Looking directly at the eyes when you make a request can also help to increase persuasiveness. But there are other features of appearance:

Changing the size of the pupil: Although it cannot be controlled, the presence of an enlarged pupil usually means that something comfortable is seen, but the constricted pupil is hostile. In any case, they are very subtle variations and are often hidden by environmental changes in light intensity. Mirroring neurons were also found to be responsible for the size that pupils adjust to that of the interactor's in an attempt to synchronize the body language to create a larger connection.

- **Raise your eyebrows:** A social greeting that means fear and lack of joy. Please don't do it in front of your favorite person.
- **Look up with your head down:** In female sex, it is considered a posture that conveys the sensuality that attracts men. In fact, many of the women's profile pictures on online dating pages are taken from above exactly (sometimes with the intention of showing the cleavage). In men, conversely, lower shots will appear higher and more dominant.
- **Maintain the appearance.** For women, establishing eye contact for 2-3 seconds before looking down is an indicator of sexual interest.

- **Flashing repeatedly:** Whether boredom or distrust, it is another way to try to block the vision of the person in front of you.
- **Look sideways.** This is another way to express boredom because you are unconsciously looking for an escape route.

4. Types of smiles

A smile is an endless source of meaning and emotion. In addition, thanks to mirror neurons, smiles are very contagious acts that can cause very positive emotions to others.

However, not only one, but in practice, you can distinguish several types of smiles depending on the content of the communication.

- Fake smiles tend to be larger on the left side of the mouth because the most specific part of the brain that primarily controls the left side of the body is in the right hemisphere.
- A natural smile (or Duchenne smile) creates wrinkles next to the eyes, raises the cheeks, and slightly lowers the eyebrows.
- A tense smile with tight lips indicates that this person does not want to share feelings with you and is a clear sign of rejection.

The biological function of smiles is to create social bonds, support trust, and eliminate the sense of threat. It has also been proven to send submissions, that is why people who want to show their power and women who want to keep their authority in a typical male professional environment avoid smiles.

5. Arm position

The arm next to the hand supports most of the movements you perform. It can also protect the most vulnerable areas of your body in situations where you feel anxious.

Propriety taught us that the communication channel between the body and mind is reciprocal. When you experience emotions, your body reflects it unconsciously, and vice versa. When you take a spontaneous posture, your mind begins to experience the associated emotions. This is especially noticeable when arms are folded.

Many people think that they cross their arms because they feel more comfortable. However, gestures are seen naturally when they match the person's attitude. Science has already shown that although gestures seem comfortable, crossing them has an important approach. Do not cross your arms when playing with friends.

These are the things you say when you take a specific position with your hands.

- **Cross arms:** Show misunderstanding and rejection. Avoid doing this unless you just want to send this message to others. In a sensual context, women usually do this when they are in the presence of men who seem too aggressive or unattractive.
- **Crossing one hand in front to hold the other hand:** Means you are not confident and have a need to feel in your arms.
- **Arms crossed with thumbs-up:** Defensive position, but at the same time wanting to express pride.
- **Joining hands in front of the genitals:** In men it provides a sense of security in situations where there is sensitivity.
- **Put your hands behind your back:** It shows confidence and fearlessness, revealing weaknesses such as the abdomen, throat, and perineum. Adopting this position in situations of uncertainty can be useful to try to gain confidence.

In general, crossing your arms means you are experiencing anxiety. Therefore, it is necessary to protect the body. There are many variations, such as adjusting the watch, placing the case in front of the body, and holding the bag in front of the chest with both hands, all of which mean the same thing.

6. *Hand gesture*

Hands, along with arms, are one of the most mobile parts of the body, providing a vast record of nonverbal communication possibilities. The most common is to use them to indicate specific parts of the body to indicate authority or gender.

It also supports verbal messages and gives them great power.

-   There is a part of the brain called the Broca region that is involved in the voice process. However, it has been proven to be activated by moving your hands. This means that the gesture is directly linked to the voice, so you can even improve your language skills by expressing yourself while doing so. Very useful for people who block when speaking in public!

-   Research also shows that if you augment phrases with gestures, the words you use come to mind first, making your message more compelling and easier to understand. The survey found that the most persuasive gestures were in line with the meaning of words, such as going back to the past.

Below you will find everything known about the meaning of hand gestures.

-   **Show open palms:** Express honesty and show the opposite when closing the fist.
-   **Hands in pockets:** Show patriotism and lack of engagement in conversations and situations.
-   **Emphasize something with your hand:** When someone offers two views with your hand, what you like most usually reinforces it with your dominant hand and palm up.
-   **Intersect fingers of both hands:** Convey a repressed, anxious, or negative attitude. If your interlocutor adopts this position, break it by giving him something so that he must hold it.
-   **Integrated fingertip:** Expresses confidence and safety, but can be confused with pride. It is very useful to detect if a rival has a good hand when playing poker.
-   **Hold the other hand.** Because it is an attempt to control oneself, it is an attempt to express frustration or hide tension.

- **Show your thumb from your pocket.** Men represent attempts to show confidence and authority over women which attracts women, but in conflict situations, they can also be a way to communicate aggression.
- **Hide only your thumb in your pocket.** It is a posture that surrounds and emphasizes the genital area. Therefore, it is a sexually open attitude that men do to show women no fear or sexual interest.
- **Put your hand on your waist.** Because he wants to increase his physical presence, he shows a slightly aggressive attitude. Many men use this to establish dominance in social circles and to look more masculine in the presence of those women that attract them. The more exposed the chest, the more active the sub-communication.

7. *Leg position*

The legs play a very interesting role in body language. Moving away from the central nervous system (brain), our rational minds can no longer control them and express greater freedom and inner feelings.

The further away your body is from your brain, the less control you have.

In general, people are programmed to get closer to what they want and get away from what they do not want. The way someone places their feet indicates where they really want to go so that they can give you the most valuable tips on nonverbal communication.

- **Advanced Feet:** The most advanced feet are almost always where you want to go. In a social situation with several people, you point to the most interesting and attractive person. If you want someone to feel attentive and emotional, make sure your feet are pointing toward him. Similarly, when the caller points to the door and not to you, it is a clear sign that you want to end the conversation.

- **Crossed legs:** A defensive and closed posture that protects the genitals. In the context of courtship, women can convey sexual rejection of men. In social situations sitting with arms and legs crossed probably means leaving the conversation. In fact, researchers Alain and Barbara Pairs conducted experiments that show that when they attend a meeting with crossed arms and legs, they don't remember the details of the meeting.

- **Sit with one foot up to the other:** Usually, a man who is competitive and ready to discuss. That would be the display version of the sitting crotch.

- **Very separate leg:** A basically masculine gesture that aims to convey dominance and territoriality.

- **Sit with curled feet:** In women, it usually means some shyness and introversion.

- **Sitting one leg side by side on the other:** This position is more squeezed and provides a younger and more sensual appearance, so if you try to pay attention to your leg, it can be interpreted as a courtship by a woman.

Learning to detect language and body language discrepancies is very helpful. Since humans cannot control all the signals they emit, what the body shows is usually very reliable.

THE 5 PRACTICAL KEYS TO MASTERING THE NONVERBAL LANGUAGE

Not only words are important to communicate and relate. Non-verbal language is decisive in most situations, in what we say and how we say it. It is the perfect accompaniment to words. It is therefore important to learn to dominate non-verbal language so as to remove the mask from words, consequently from people.

How to dominate non-verbal language
Know yourself
A key tip for mastering non-verbal language is to know yourself. It's the best way to get information about yourself, to know who we really are.

That is to say, if we focus well, we can observe who we really are. What does it mean that you touch an eye? Think about what is happening at that moment in your mind so you will know why you expressed that typical act of non-verbal language.

It may seem like a simple exercise, but it is absolutely not the case. However, it will become very useful in every area of your life, because the more one knows, the more chance one will have of transforming one's existence into what one really wants.

> *"People often say they haven't found themselves yet. But the self is not something that is found but that is created."*
>
> *-Thomas Szasz-*

The face reflects the soul
They say that the face is the mirror of the soul, its true reflection. There are certainly people capable of dominating non-verbal language so as not to show others what is going on in their minds and their right mood. In general, however, we can learn a lot about them through people's faces and expressions.

The face has a vast number of facial muscles, with extraordinary functions. They show our right mood. There is even science that bases its theories on facial features; it's called morphopsychology. It is therefore clear that thanks to one's face, you can know a lot about a person.

How can you practice such facial gestures to dominate non-verbal language and avoid the externalization of emotions? This is a challenging practice. The face and its musculature were created to show elemental emotions such as anger, sadness, surprise, or joy. Each of them involves several mechanisms. Mastering them is a difficult task.
In this sense, when you dominate a non-verbal language, the only thing you can do to avoid showing emotions is to fake them. It would be like hiding real feelings.

It would be good to look at yourself in the mirror for a long time until you manage to dominate your statements. For example, if you feel joy, put your sad expression on your face, exercising with the muscles that are activated when you display any emotions until you can control them.

Look in the eyes
A good technique to master non-verbal language is to look directly into the eyes. We must not forget that constantly avoiding the eyes of others shows terrible insecurity and lack of self-confidence.
Looking directly into the eyes of the interlocutor, on the other hand, gives the feeling of participating in a conversation between peers, showing less of themselves. It is an important piece to dominate non-verbal language since in this way you only externalize what you really want to show to the other person.

Be natural
To dominate non-verbal language, nothing works like behaving in a natural way, being yourself. The more you know yourself, the less you will worry about showing something undesirable. In this sense, it will become easier to establish relationships with other people and you will have no worries about what you will show or not through your gestures.
Learn to be yourself, to emphasize the movements that are proper to your person, avoiding the mannerisms and elements that do not belong to your true nature. Those acquired vices are easily interpreted by others.

Keep calm

To appear relaxed, in full calm, is a simple form of dominating the non-verbal language. Anxiety, nerves or anger lead us to externalize our way of being too much through gestures and face.

*"A man who finds no satisfaction
in himself will seek it in vain
elsewhere."*

-La Rochefoucauld-

BODY LANGUAGE AND EMOTIONS

In this 21st century, we are experiencing a scientific revolution based on an emerging science: neurosciences. They help us understand how emotional processes and non-verbal language expressions occur.

Definition "emotional"
The semantic meaning of the word emotion comes from Latin:

e-motio = movement towards

This implies that emotion is life; it is movement, direction, it implies some physical reaction that moves the body. That's it, body language.

The definition of the emotion is "intense and fleeting mood alteration that is accompanied by a certain somatic shock." This means that the emotion:

- Implies an alteration or change.
- Is associated with mood, our ability to perceive, feel and act.
- Can be intense or short.
- Creates a change or reaction of a somatic type, that is, in the physical body.

At the moment, we see that emotions are taking shape in the body and create certain changes. These signals can be read in body language and are often emotionally based.

Other different concepts that are often confused with emotion are:

- Feeling
- Temperament
- Drive
- Instinct
- Impulse
- Passion
- Wish
- Cheer up
- Attitude

Detecting the emotions of others is essential in social interactions. On one hand, they serve as an explanation for past and present behaviors. On the other hand, they guide our expectations regarding future actions. Thus, we infer emotions that others feel and express, and these inferences (along with other factors) shape our social responses.

Is it our emotions and our way of interpreting life that determine our posture? Or is it the postures that condition our emotions and our interpretation?

Posture which is a strategy used by our neuromuscular and skeletal systems to remain in balance in the most economical way possible, is also our way of being in the world. With our musculoskeletal system, we express our emotions, and with it, we express ourselves in general.

Thus, it is essential to re-educate our posture and make ourselves aware of it to improve our emotional part and vice versa. The daily body language of each of us represents and exacerbates our emotions and our state of mind. When we release a muscular-emotional charge held for a long time, one immediately feels release. If we emotionally hold back or don't pay attention to it, the emotional energy turns into muscle, joint, or respiratory tension.

We will make a summary of four key emotional movements as FEAR, ANGER/RAGE, JOY, AND SADNESS.

-    Fear closes our posture, generating slower breathing and a general lack of muscular strength. It generates a feeling of weakness and of not being able to face life.
-    Rage/aggressiveness/anger excessively opens our posture with faster breathing and an increase in the dynamic muscles' tone. It generates constant muscular tension and rigidity (more prone to contractures).
-    Joy gives us good breath, lets us inspire, and oxygenate ourselves. It generates an upright and fluid posture in turn.
-    Sadness rolls our whole body down as if we had completely disconnected from our body. Think of the phrase "your spirits fall to the ground." Therefore, this necessary emotion at certain times will induce us to breathe without force.

These four emotions are necessary and vital in a moderate way and at the right time to optimally face our day to day. The problem arises if we constantly live in one of them.

There is a somato-psycho-emotional balance point among these four. That is why it is essential to be in it to feel in harmony with ourselves, breathe fluidly, and consequently avoid certain bodily pains in the short term. In the long term, there are other more serious dysfunctions or pathologies. It should be taken into account that each person has a specific somato-psycho-emotional pattern that generates a bodily imbalance. In this imbalance or deviation, emphasis should be placed on a physiotherapeutic level, developing certain tools for the patient to avoid a series of alterations at the joint, muscular, and respiratory level.

We must never forget that when there is back pain, there is emotional suffering.

HOW TO READ BODY LANGUAGE

Knowing how to interpret another person's body language has a closer relationship because non-verbal communication accounts for up to 60% of all interpersonal communication. Therefore, paying attention to the signals sent through the body language and interpreting them successfully is a very useful skill. With a little care, you can learn to decipher these cues correctly and practice hard to make this habit instinct.

1. Interpreting emotional signs
Be careful not to cry because we believe that most cultures are caused by emotional explosions. Tears are often seen as a sign of suffering and sorrow, but they are not only manifested through laughter and humor but are also expressions of happiness. Therefore, you need to look at other signs to determine the proper context for tears.

- A person may force or manipulate a cry to gain empathy or to deceive others. This practice is known as "crocodile tears". An informal expression based on the myth of "crying" when a crocodile catches prey.

Watch for signs of anger and threats. Threat signs include a V-shaped eyebrow, wide eyes, open mouth, or lower lip corners.

- A tightly crossed arm is a common sign of irritation and rejection.

Watch for signs of anxiety. When anxiety occurs, people blink more, face movement increases, and lips stretch to form thin lines.

- Anxious people lose their composure and can move their hands over and over without stopping.
- Another way to show anxiety is to step and move your feet unconsciously.

Note the embarrassing expression. We smile and show embarrassment in a controlled or tense manner, looking away, or turning the head sideways.

- If you look too much at the floor, you are very likely to be shy or embarrassed. You look down when you're upset or want to hide your emotions. When people spend a lot of time looking at the floor, they usually think bad things and experience uncomfortable feelings.

Observe the expression of pride. Individuals show pride by carefully smiling, tilting their heads back and placing their hands on their hips.

2. Interpretation of interpersonal signs

Assess distance and proximity: These are ways to communicate the status of interpersonal relationships. Touch and physical proximity show love and affection.

- Two people in an intimate relationship require less personal space than two strangers.
- It is important to note that personal spaces are culturally fluid. So keep in mind that what is considered nearby in one country may be considered far in another.

Please read people's eyes. According to research, if an individual has an interesting conversation, they may see the caller's face for about 80% of the time. However, the focus is not only on the eyes, but the line of sight sometimes moves to the lips and nose and may face downward, but is always placed on the other person's eyes.

- Usually, when someone looks up to the right during a conversation, they are bored and not interested in speaking.
- Inflated pupils are interested in what is happening. However, be aware that many substances can cause this expansion, such as alcohol, cocaine, amphetamine, and LSD.

- Eye contact is also widely used to show integrity. Too much or aggressiveness with someone's eyes suggests that you are very aware of the message you want to convey. Therefore, if an individual does not want to lie and appear to avoid the interlocutor, he can intentionally change the way he maintains eye contact. This is a famous sign of a lie. However, as stated earlier, take into account the various individual differences in associating eye contact with lies.

Observe the posture. The person who puts his arm behind his neck or head gives a message that he is speaking or perhaps that he is generally a relaxed individual.

- The tight crossing of arms and legs often indicates resistance and poor acceptability. In general, when we adopt this stance, we inform others that we are mentally, emotionally and physically closed.
- In a study where 2,000 transactions were recorded on videotape to assess the negotiator's body language, no transaction was made with one of the participants crossed.

3. Interpretation of signs of attraction

Analyze eye contact. Watching someone's eyes is a sign of attraction because it flashes 6 to 10 times a minute than the normal average.

- Keep in mind that flashing is a flickering or attractive sign, but this is not true for all cultures. Some Asians are frustrated with the wink and consider it rude.

Pay attention to certain facial expressions. Since smiles are one of the clearest signs of attraction, you will learn to decipher forced smiles from real smiles. We know that smiles are false when it doesn't move the corners of the eyes. True smiles often cause wrinkles in the corners of the eyes (wrinkled legs). Wrinkles do not appear when people laugh.

- Raising the eyebrows is another sign related to flirting.

Consider the person's gesture and posture. In general, individuals tend to approach the people they are attracted to. They may lean against you or may be more direct and touch you. Lightly touching or stroking someone's arm is a sign of attraction.

- They are also interested in turning their feet forward to attracted people.
- An upward-facing palm suggests acceptability and is another indicator of love interest.

Don't forget the gender difference. Men and women can show physical attraction in a variety of ways.

- Men lean forward and can turn their torso towards those who are interested. Meanwhile, a woman who meets his intentions pulls his torso apart and leans back.
- A man in love with someone can raise his hand over his head at a 90-degree angle.
- When a woman expresses her charm, she can touch her body with her hand in the area between her waist and chin, with her arms open.

4.   Interpreting power signals

Pay attention to eye contact. If you look at it, the movement communication channel is the main way to convey control. Those who want to prove authority have the freedom to face and evaluate others while maintaining direct eye contact. They will also be the last people to suspend eye contact.

- If you want to exercise power, keep in mind that constant eye contact can intimidate others.

Evaluate facial expressions. If you think seriously, those who want to show an advantage can avoid smiles and squeeze their lips.

Analyze gestures and postures. Gestures can show superiority. Pointing at others and making many gestures is a way to show power. It also shows superiority when someone is relaxed but at the same time maintains a higher posture than others and occupies more body space.

- The dominant individual also has a very firm handshake. To show control, they often hang up with their hands up and greet with a firm and lasting grip.

Consider how someone controls your space. A high person generally maintains a larger physical space when interacting with a lower person. Authoritarians often occupy more space to express the rule of the situation. In other words, a vast attitude shows success and power.

- It also works when you decide to stand instead of sitting. Standing up (especially in front of everyone) is considered a posture of power.
- Furthermore, rather than bend forward, you can increase your confidence by keeping your back straight and keeping your shoulders back. A sloppy posture that already leans forward conveys anxiety.
- The dominant individual also guides the rest of the group, walking in front of everyone and first through the door. They like to be in front.

Notice how and when people touch other people. Those who show superiority are so confident that they easily touch other people. In general, in situations where one person has more authority than another, the most powerful individuals tend to touch the lower position person more often. In social situations where both parties are in the same position, people respond to the ring in a similar manner.

5.   Understanding body language
Note that the interpretation of body language is a complex task. Nonverbal behavior is complex. Because we are all different and appear in the world in various ways. Reading body language can be difficult because it requires a general context to be able to interpret the received signal. For example, was this person fighting with his wife or saying he could not be promoted? Was she visibly anxious at lunch?

- Whenever possible, when interpreting someone's body language, you need to consider their personality and language behavior, social factors, and the surrounding environment. Such information is not always available but can be very helpful in reading body language. Because people are complex, communicating in complex ways through the body is natural!

- Compare the habits of reading body language and watching your favorite TV show. In addition to watching program scenes, you can understand the meaning of the problem scene correctly and understand the entire episode. You are also very likely to remember past episodes, character stories, and the entire plot. When interpreting body language, you should also pay attention to the overall context!

Remember that nonverbal communication varies from culture to culture. Some emotions and expressions in body language have culturally specific meanings.

- People with certain conditions such as the autism spectrum may behave differently, such as not being able to see the caller while listening.
- For example, in Finnish culture, people are receptive to seeing their eyes. On the other hand, eye contact is considered to be a sign of Japanese anger.
- Another example: In Western cultures, when you are comfortable, they lean on you and leave their face and body facing you.
- Keep in mind that although specific expressions of emotion vary from culture to culture, some studies have shown that specific expressions of body language are universal. This is especially true for domination and submission communication. For example, in many different cultures, maintaining a curved posture indicates obedience.

Note that the interpretation depends on the communication channel. In non-language channels, messages or signals are sent without words. The most important non-verbal channels include movement forms (eye contact, facial expression, body language), tactile (touch), and proxyomic (personal space) communication. That is, the media determines the message.

- As a rule, it is easy to interpret facial expressions, followed by body language, followed by touch and personal space.

- There are several variations within each channel. For example, not all facial expressions are equally easy to understand, but there is a tendency to read comfortable facial expressions rather than unpleasant facial expressions. One study shows that people can better interpret signs of happiness, joy, and excitement compared to anger, sadness, fear, and disgust.

CHAPTER TEN

OPTIMISTIC AND PESSIMISTIC PEOPLE

Optimism or pessimism are best understood from the comparison of those attitudes of each point of view. The same person can go through moments of optimism and others of greater pessimism in their own life. However, when each human being looks with sincerity inside, he can also realize what is the most common tendency in his life or in his presence. What are the characteristics of optimistic and pessimistic people?

How does an optimistic person act?
Optimism produces admiration since most people want to live it in practice. However, optimism is not innate but is cultivated through habits marked by constancy. How does an optimistic person act?

1. Sense of humor
They are people who have the ability to relativize external difficulties and circumstances through a funny look that puts the spotlight on some comic aspect of reality itself. The sense of humor is a personal decision since each person can cultivate it individually.

2. Observe things in context
In relation to the previous point, optimistic people are also able to relativize certain circumstances because they attend to the context of what happened and observe that everything happens and nothing remains. That is to say, what today is fully topical, in just a few days will be passed. Therefore, optimists live the present with a constructive vision.

3. Authenticity
True optimism is only effective when it is sincere. From this perspective, one of the character faces of optimistic people is that they radiate light where they are because they spread their good energy to others through reflections, words, and attitudes.

4. Realistic

Sometimes those who live a life of pessimism feel that optimists move away from reality in their interpretations. However, truly effective positive thinking is one that also integrates the reality of life. Optimistic people also experience difficulties and difficult times. However, they try to focus on dealing with what they can manage instead of worrying chronically. They try to generate alternatives, they look for help if they need it and they don't lock themselves up.

5. Emotional well-being

Much of the well-being that optimistic people experience depends on their own attitude. That is, this sense of harmony is a reflection of the positive impact that happy thoughts produce on the emotional level through a friendly and constructive inner dialogue. The optimist has a constructive self-image of himself and the way in which he observes influences the way he positions himself in the different spheres of his life.

What does it mean to be a pessimistic person?

Optimistic people also have moments of pessimism. And those who feel more pessimistic have moments of optimism. For this reason, both concepts feedback on the experience of living itself. The main difference between optimism and pessimism may be the way of approaching life and the challenges that it proposes. What are the characteristics of people who tend to think negative?

1. The negative view of reality

This can be observed in all-time fragments. For example, the protagonist remembers more frequently the sad situations of yesterday or lives with the perception of chronic longing that prevents him from enjoying the present. In the same way, he focuses more on the shortcomings than on the reasons for gratitude for the present. Similarly, he visualizes the future from the prism of insecurity. Therefore, pessimism, like optimism, shows a look at reality.

2. Frequent complaints

If in the plane of thought there are limiting beliefs that boycott the potential of that person, in the plane of verbal expression the tendency to complain arises as a response of personal dissatisfaction. The complaint does not solve anything by itself, however, it seems a mantra for those who contemplate reality from the perspective of self-pity, the feeling of bad luck, comparison with others or fear. Sometimes, pessimistic people conclude that they have no luck because this is the message that they have repeated to themselves on countless occasions.

3. They have a wrong picture of themselves
Pessimistic people have a distorted view of their abilities and talent. And often they confuse the way they see themselves with the way they think they are seen by others. For example, they don't feel comfortable when they receive words of recognition because they don't think they really deserve it. Pessimism is one of the characteristics of people with low self-esteem.

4. They are compared with others
Pessimistic people can lose doses of energy in the recurring tendency to live from comparison by idealizing others and placing themselves in the role of inferiority.

5. Insecurity
There are so many negative thoughts that can go through the mind of a person throughout a single day that these beliefs are transferred to the plane of action in the form of an attitude marked by insecurity in new situations that produce fear.

How to become an optimistic person
Optimism and pessimism are not absolute concepts since every human being has negative and positive thoughts. The characteristics of optimistic and pessimistic people can appear in the same individual simultaneously. So, the question, "Is it better to be optimistic or pessimistic?" sometimes may not make much sense.

How to have an optimistic attitude

However, if a person feels that the weight of negativity considerably exceeds the good energy of optimism, then he can commit to his own ability to initiate a process of personal change because optimism is not an exclusive privilege of those who feel this way, but a possible and attainable goal. How to become an optimistic person?

- Just as there is no definitive limit on wisdom, there is no maximum limit on optimism. Therefore, try to value those simple day-to-day actions that you exercise in order to take care of yourself.
- Decide to be optimistic. To do this, make a list of reasons why you want to achieve this mission. These reasons constitute an important source of your motivation. When you face a complex situation, remember that you are free to decide how you want to respond to it. Which option compensates you the most? Choose the one that suits you best.
- Personal growth courses. As important as professional training is life training. And these self-knowledge workshops can mark a turning point in those who run new resources and resilience skills in the context of training sessions guided by experts in psychology.
- Bring humor to your life through cinema, theater, monologues, literature and conversations with friends. The stimulation of humor sharpens your ingenuity for the benefit of happiness.

If you want to change your life, start by changing your attitude.

CHAPTER ELEVEN

COLD PEOPLE AND CALCULATORS: MOST COMMON FEATURES

In society, there are many people, so there are also very different ways of being. Ways of being that can be more or less compatible with your character and the way you live life. There is a way of being that is quite difficult to cope with: there are cold people and calculators who never lose control of situations, have a low level of empathy, and listen more to their thoughts than their emotions ... What can you do in case you have to be near someone like that?

What to do before a cold and calculating person?
First, try to see the good of that person. Everyone has positive points and defects, so it is worth learning to live by focusing attention on the friendlier side of others. On the other hand, you decide the degree of privacy you want to have with each person. There are more superficial relationships than others, so it may not be the most appropriate to have a cold and calculating person as a close friend.

You have to keep in mind that a person who has this personality, surely, has developed in this way due to a lack of love and affection during his stage of development and growth. The truth is that, usually, people who are this way tend to suffer great emotional deficiencies and, therefore, their coldness and attitude towards the world are created in the form of a "shield" to protect themselves from possible attacks that they may receive from the rest.

It is important to understand why a person is cold and calculating and, in these cases, instead of leaving him aside, try to help him so that he may feel that not everyone is going to hurt him. After all, this type of personality develops as a defense against an attack he received in the past, so it can be modified.

How are cold people: the 6 most outstanding features

The personality of cold people and calculators can also be associated with other non-positive traits: emotional blackmail, manipulation, or use of people based on their own interests... It is not bad to be cold at certain times in life, in fact, it is very positive to be in business, for example. However, someone who behaves like this does not always let things flow by pure inertia, he does not relax.

People who are cold mark a barrier that you cannot overcome. This barrier is invisible, however, you really feel it, therefore whoever has to live with that barrier for a long time may have tension and discomfort from an inner stiffness that prevents him from being natural. People who are cold and calculating can change, but they will only do so at their own wish.

Next, we will discover the characteristics of cold people and calculators so you can learn to detect if, around you, there is someone who acts in this way:

- **Traumas of the past:** As we have said in the previous section, it is most likely that this person is this way because of a bad experience lived in the past. His attitude appears as a defense, a shield to avoid being harmed.
- **Very rational people:** A calculating person never gets carried away by feelings. They are usually people with a very analytical view of life and who, before taking a false step, have valued in detail everything that can happen next.
- **Very intelligent:** Normally, people who meet these characteristics are also very intelligent. The constant use of reason means that they can establish stereotypes of people and know how they are going to act, something that allows them to anticipate the facts or even manipulate them.
- **They don't talk too much:** Another characteristic of cold people and calculators is that they are not very prone to talk and communicate. They prefer to be silent and observe, analyze the different behaviors of people and then act in relation to it. They are usually introverted.

- **Distrustful:** It is one of the most common characteristics of these people and they do not trust anyone. This is probably due to the bad experiences of his past that made him become a distrustful person and afraid that others would harm him. Therefore, these people live somewhat evaded from society, they may have friends, yes, but they will intimate very little with them, or establish superficial relationships for fear that others may hurt or take advantage of their weaknesses.
- **Pessimists:** And finally, a cold person is also usually pessimistic, because he believes that everyone wants and can take advantage of others. Instead of seeing the beautiful side of the human being, he has him in very low regard and sees him as a social "wolf" rather than as a person wanting to do well and to relate positively.

How to be a cold person - tips

If once you know how cold people act, you feel that your personality is quite the opposite and that it would not hurt to be a little colder in some moments or areas of your life, take note of the advice listed below with the knowledge that you can get to be a colder person and avoid everything that happens to you affecting you in excess:

- Focus all your attention on the future and what you can do from now on to improve your life. A person with a colder mind continually thinks about what can change and does not remain anchored in the past which, in short, are past events or events that cannot be changed.
- You must start to be a more methodical person, that is, establish certain plans to follow to achieve all your life goals and objectives. Dedication, perseverance and determination are the elements that can help you have better performance and achieve what you set your mind to.
- Be a more independent person. It's okay to help and please others, but perhaps you need to think a little more about yourself and focus, first, on your needs. It is also important that you make your own decisions based on your desires and reasoning and that you learn to enjoy loneliness, understanding that it also has its positive points.

- If you are a very outgoing person, you tend to be the one who directs all conversations and accounts with a great facility to explain your personal problems to others, you can try to be a little more reserved from now on. Before speaking, try to organize your thoughts and determine if that is the right moment or you are in front of the right person to give that information.

CHARACTERISTICS OF AN ALPHA PERSON
Have you heard of the existence of alpha people? Both women and men can be considered as "alpha", a term that refers to the leadership capacity, independence and strength that each can have. It is usually a qualification that is used in the animal environment (the alpha male of the pack), however, currently it is also used to define people with specific qualities.

CHARACTERISTICS AND TRAITS OF AN ALPHA MALE
There has been a lot of talk about alpha males; however, do you know exactly what their most characteristic features are? Here we are going to discover the 5 characteristics of an alpha male so you can understand how they are.

He does not give up in the face of adversity
One of the main characteristics of an alpha person is that they do not give up in the face of life's complications. They are usually people who, no matter how bad things go, do not give up. They are, therefore, fighters, persistent and with great courage to overcome any obstacle they may experience in their lives.

The alpha male is brave
The alpha male is also usually a brave person. He is very clear about what he wants in life and, therefore, will fight with nails and teeth to get it. He is not afraid of problems and, if at any time in doubt, brings out all his courage to overcome any fear.

Leadership spirit
An alpha male is also characterized because he is usually a born leader. He is usually the singing voice in numerous groups of people, he is also usually very respected and with a very firm opinion of life and any situation. His sympathy, extroversion and self-confidence make him, easily, become the leader of groups of people, even when he is new to that environment.

Ambitious and competitive people

Alpha also tend to be people who have very clear goals and will fight, with nails and teeth, to achieve them. They are ambitious people who want to scale and improve both their knowledge and their professional and personal life. This trait of ambition means that they, too, can be competitive people when they have to fight for their own goals.

Self-confidence

And finally, another characteristic of alpha men is that they tend to have great confidence in themselves. They know what they want and go for it. They feel strong and brave to achieve it, therefore, there is nothing in their path that can intrude and change their destiny. They tend to have very clear ideas and be comfortable with their personality and their way of seeing life.

The personality of the alpha woman: highlights

We continue with this section with the characteristics of an alpha person to talk now about the features of women. There are alpha women and, like men, they are strong, independent, brave and self-confident women. But, so that you know them better, we will discover the most outstanding features of this type of women.

Independent women

Alpha women are characterized because they are very independent. They don't need anyone to be happy, they alone are complete and satisfied. The people around her are there because she wants them to be there, that is, there is no need or attachment in their relationships. They are women who live their life the way they want to do it and who do not seek the approval of anything or anyone.

She knows what she wants

An alpha woman is also very clear about what she wants from life. And goes for it. She has no qualms about setting high goals and struggling to achieve them. They are usually people with a high degree of self-confidence and strong convictions.
Although, like everyone else, they may have more or less good periods, in general they are people who know what they want to achieve.

Ambitious and persistent

Another characteristic of an alpha person is that there is nothing to resist them. In the case of women, they are ambitious and have no small dreams: they go big. In addition, even if there is something that is slightly complicated, they will fight and continue to persist until they achieve their goals.

They love and respect themselves
It is also an obvious sign in an alpha woman who has high self-esteem. That is, they are people who love themselves, respect themselves and will never harm themselves. This makes them know how to avoid toxic or destructive relationships and that they put themselves before anyone who may not do them well. They are strong, self-confident and with tremendous courage.

They learn from mistakes
Alpha women are usually people with a high degree of self-knowledge, so they do not give up in the face of any mistake nor do they get angry at it. They try to bring learning to each situation and keep growing with life's lessons. They know that they don't always win but they always learn, so, no matter how much they make a mistake or make bad decisions, they will always know how to redirect their lives again.

Alpha, beta and omega personality
As a summary, we will now analyze the 3 types of personalities that exist in society. We will talk about the characteristics of an alpha person but also about beta and omega. In this way, you can know better your profile or identify them in your circle of family or friends.

Alpha personality
As we have already said, alpha people are characterized by being brave, independent, strong, self-confident and ambitious. They are self-sufficient people who do not usually need anything from anyone to be happy. Here is a list of the most common characteristics of these people:
- Self-confidence
- High security
- High self-esteem
- Leadership spirit
- Independence
- Ambitious and competitive people

Beta personality

There are not only alpha people in the world but there are also other personalities that are also worth knowing. This is the case of beta people, that is, people who have some alpha traits but, also, are a bit more docile. Here you have a list with the most common characteristics:

- Very imaginative people
- They are brave but cautious: they will analyze the situation well before making a decision
- Responsible persons
- They are constant and do not give up at the first exchange
- They have a more sensitive personality than alpha

Omega personality

In the world of animals, the omega is that living being that is governed by the rules of the two previous personalities: the alpha and the omega. However, they have a very specific personality and full of details that we will analyze below:

- They are people in love
- They get carried away by the most leading people
- They are usually insecure people who have trouble making decisions
- They are very outgoing and with many friends
- They have a rather calm and relaxed life

CHAPTER TWELVE

PSYCHOLOGICAL PROFILE OF AN UNFAITHFUL PERSON

Infidelity can refer to concrete action in a person's life or, on the contrary, be a repeated attitude in the sentimental biography of the protagonist that repeats a similar scheme in each new relationship. This is one of the characteristics repeated in the profile of an unfaithful person. The fact of having starred in a similar episode on different occasions shows a concept of love in which a relationship is compatible with another parallel link (from the point of view of the infidel). Each person is different, however, there are some common characteristics. What is the psychological profile of an unfaithful person?

Constant seduction

Within the psychological profile of an unfaithful person it should be noted that, in general, it is usually a person to like and feel desired. And, especially, when the monotony has arrived at the love story, that incentive of desire that activates his sensations arises. In this case, seduction is lived intensely by being at the limit of what feels forbidden or hidden from others.

Falling into temptation is an incentive for novelty in the life of the protagonist who struggles not to be discovered. And, something that defines the psychological profile of the unfaithful person is that they do not want to give up these short stories, but they also do not want this fact to come to light before the risk of abandonment by their partner.

Generally, an unfaithful person does not observe reality in a democratic way. While he wants to have the freedom to live more than one story, he does not live with the same predisposition that his partner may have a relationship with another person. Justify infidelity and find excuses to act in this way. Live reality from the supremacy of the self, that is, from the ego.

Look for that feeling of passion that allows you to experience the frequent feelings of sentimental idealization where each one observes the other as perfect. Feel difficult to face a routine stage in a relationship when the butterflies have been left behind in the stomach or the intensity of the first dates without having that incentive of emotions so alive.

Vulnerable Self-Esteem
The psychological profile of an unfaithful person also often means that their self-esteem depends, largely, on that search for external approval in that game of seduction that is born from the desire to like and feel desired in the eyes of others. Therefore, this hides fragile self-confidence.
In turn, this search for the reaffirmation of one's own personal attractiveness through the language of seduction in a story external to the couple's relationship also connects with a need for constant youth before the law of the passage of time that produces a visible effect on body image.
The person temporarily covers possible emotional deficiencies and internal voids, however, beyond the surface is the suffering that produces emotional dependence. Although the infidel is very free to make decisions of this kind, in reality, he is very conditioned by his own habits and beliefs.

Permanent deception
Frequent infidelities are a symptom of the lack of transparency that a person has to talk about himself with his partner. Lying is a common resource to disguise reality. He who feels cheated may discover some contradiction in the versions given on a subject, notice sudden behavioral changes in his partner's lifestyle, or observe inconsistent excuses to be absent from important celebrations.

Although what defines an unfaithful person is not only his ability to lie, but also, the naturalness with which he does and how convincing it can be if his partner does not distrust his actions yet. If at any time there is a definitive break when discovered, a new relationship will begin soon because this sentimental dependence makes the protagonist feel uncomfortable with the idea of loneliness.

Therefore, behind the profile of an unfaithful person there is also an internal fear of that feeling of emptiness that arises from the experience of feeling alone without having chosen it.

PSYCHOLOGICAL PROFILE OF A LIAR

While it is true that almost all of us have ever lied in our lives (even if it is a little white lie), there are people who do it again and again, as if they could not stop or find it hard to face the truth itself. These types of individuals inspire little confidence and make us feel insecure about whether what they feel and what they tell us is true or is another lie.

A liar can have this attitude for many reasons, however, it usually follows a pattern quite similar to that of other individuals with a tendency to tell lies. Is it possible to make the psychological profile of a liar?

Attitudes of a liar
First, it is important to know that lying sometimes in our lives does not mean that we are pathological liars. In fact, we are likely to remember that time when we did not want to tell our friend that that shirt fit badly, or when we prefer to tell our mother that what she had cooked was delicious even if it was not. White lies are part of our daily lives and although they are not honest behaviors, they are not always the reflection of a high lying person.

The problem begins to arise when our attitudes are based on lying to everyone around us. Telling a white lie on one occasion is not bad, however, lying again and again about many of the elements that surround us is a sign of danger. These types of attitudes must be identified to be able to change them through personal growth exercises and even psychological therapy if necessary.

How a liar acts
Next, we will make a list of behaviors to be able to elaborate a complete psychological profile of a liar:
- Usually a person insecure and with low self-esteem, believes that what surrounds him is not enough and that, for that reason, should elaborate lies about his life.
- He doesn't talk much (for lack of elaboration of the lie) or, on the contrary, he develops an extensive unreal story and talks all the time about it.

- The liar when he is discovered becomes angry or becomes the victim, thus diverting the attention from the lie and projecting it towards anger or sadness.
- Once someone discovers his lie, he will continue to deny it until his story is no longer held anywhere.
- Some experts claim that making many hand gestures is also a sign that a person is lying.
- A person with a lack of empathy for others is more likely to be a liar.
- It can also be characterized either by impulsivity (lying as a response reflects the fear of being judged) or, on the contrary: for being a cold and calculating person who lies in a very elaborate way.

HOW TO FIND OUT IF SOMEONE LIES TO YOU

As we have seen, the psychology of a liar is very complicated and depends on many factors, each person can lie for one reason or another and, if we do not know the individual well, unmasking a liar can become very complicated.
If we want to find out if a person lies or not, we can try to ask him questions about a particular fact that arouses suspicion. Let's give an example:

Your friend tells you that he has a wonderful job after years without looking for a job, however, you don't end up believing it. You can start asking him the following questions: "And what is your job?" "How long have you been there?" "What are the names of your colleagues?" ... if you see that they have to think about the questions or answer differently each time someone asks them, it is possible that that person is lying to us.

Another way to unmask a hoax is knowing if a person lies by their gestures.

Can a liar change?

Although at first glance it seems like a very complicated task, all people change and evolve if they are firmly proposed. Lying is a behavior, not an invariable personality style. It is true that there will be people who have more difficulties to stop lying, however, it is not impossible.

Pathological liars: treatment

While it is true that we all have the opportunity to change our behaviors and stop telling lies, there is a group of individuals that this task can cost enormously: pathological liars.

What disorder does a liar have?

There is a psychological disorder called mythomania that is characterized by a lack of control over lies. A mythomaniac usually lies compulsively, making stories parallel to his real life. This disease can develop from small deceptions that end up leading to an intricate network of compulsive and pathological lies.

The treatment of mythomania is totally psychological. To perform a therapeutic intervention the first step will be to develop your own psychological profile, secondly, it will be necessary to treat your social skills, your self-esteem (pillar of your lies and insecurities) and, finally, perform exercises that put into practice your ability to tell the truth.

Avoiding lying is much simpler than sustaining a parallel life based on deception. With the truth ahead, we show the world our most real and honest face, that is a sign of maturity and good personal abilities. If we get the pathological liar to see these values, it will be much simpler for him to heal and lead a life free of lies.

HOW TO KNOW IF A PERSON LIES BY THEIR GESTURES

There are different ways to realize when a person is hiding something from us and even when he is not telling us the truth. When we tell the truth we don't have to make too much effort to remember and express what happened, however when we are going to tell a lie, our brain has to make an extra effort to hide from the other person and to create that fictional story that we are going to communicate.

How to know if someone lies by the eyes
They say that the eyes are the window of the soul and that is when it comes to identifying if a friend is false and is lying or not, the expression and movement of his eyes can tell us a lot about it.

For example, when a person prefers not to look you in the eye when he is telling you something and tries to dodge your gaze, he lowers it and turns to see everywhere, except you, that person effectively is lying to you. On the other hand, it has been found and this is something that is widely used in neurolinguistic programming, that people who look to the right side when they are telling you something is because they are telling the truth, however when they look to the left side it can be a great indicator that they are lying.

But why does this happen? What happens is that the information we want to obtain is found in different areas of our brain, for example the area where that information about the events that happened in the past is stored is different from the area where we consciously want to create new information that in this case would be the lie. This is why we tend to look at different sites when we are trying to communicate something. It may also be that a person who normally does not have any nervous tic, begins to do something with their eyes, whether they are closed and opened constantly or that their eyes are very different, which is better perceived if we know that person well in advance.

Attitudes of a liar
Although a person tends to lie frequently, unless he is an expert in the subject and in the art of acting, we can generally predict it in a relatively simple way if we have enough knowledge of how to do it.

However, despite this, we can never 100% affirm that this person really lies since it is somewhat more subjective and we have to analyze the whole context in general. Here are the most common attitudes of a liar:

- They tend to be slow in their speech because while they are preparing it, they are also thinking that this is what they are going to tell you.
- They repeat a lot of the questions you ask them to give themselves more time to elaborate the lie.
- They talk too many rodeos, there tends to be little direction as to what they want to communicate.
- They can be corrected often because they tell different stories to each person, so they often do not remember what they have said in the past.
- When they are asked something in particular, they do not give a specific answer, they try to confuse the person who is asking them the question and finally answer something different from what they were asked or simply do not answer and try to leave by the tangent.

Signs that someone is lying

There are currently several studies that have shown how we can detect if a person is lying only through their gestures. It is clear that in most cases nonverbal communication can express more than verbal communication and it is easier to analyze a person through this type of communication and not based solely on what he says:

- **Changes in body posture.** When they are telling you what they want to tell you and especially when they realize that you can fall for them, they change their body posture sharply. For example, they may be sitting with their legs open and crossing them quickly, starting to stroke their hair, closing their arms, etc.
- **Changes in the tone of voice.** The tone of voice is another extremely important factor when detecting a lie. When a person lies, at the moment he begins to do so, his voice tone changes considerably, he may start talking with many pauses, his voice cracking, his voice rising or decreasing, etc.

- **That his gestures do not match what he says.** It may be that when the person is telling you the lie, in this case, their gestures do not match what they are communicating to you. For example, a person who says he feels sad for some situation or bothers but his facial and even body gestures show the opposite, that he is relaxed and calm.
- **Blushing.** This usually happens a lot to people who are not used to lying and trying to do so. So it may be that when the person comes to talk to you to tell you the lie (if it is) begins to blush.
- **Rigid posture.** When someone lies, they are generally not going to find themselves relaxed, so their body stiffness that will be evident can be a great indicator that they are lying to us.

www.ingramcontent.com/pod-product-compliance
Lightning Source LLC
Chambersburg PA
CBHW050736030426
42336CB00012B/1600